THE BEST POLITICAL CARTOONS OF THE YEAR 2009 EDITION

DARYL CAGLE MSNBC.COM

Dedication

For all those editorial cartoonists who are losing their jobs, as our profession evolves into a hobby.

The Best Political Cartoons of the Year, 2009 Edition

Daryl Cagle, Cartoonist-Editor, Front Cover
Brian Fairrington, Cartoonist-Editor, Back Cover
Susie Cagle, Writer
Laura Norman, Executive Editor for Que Publishing
Thanks to our Cagle Cartoons staff for their contributions: Stacey Fairrington, Cari Dawson Bartley, Bob Bartley and Brian Davis.

Special thanks to: Tribune Media Services, United Media and Creators Syndicate.

ISBN-13: 978-0-7897-3815-8
ISBN-10: 0-7897-3815-5
Library of Congress Cataloging-in-Publication data is on file.
Printed in the United States of America
First Printing: December 2008

THE BEST POLITICAL CARTOONS OF THE YEAR 2009 EDITION

Table of Contents

About this book

This was a wild year for editorial cartoonists! There was too much news! The economy crashed; we had a wild campaign season and the election of the first African American President; gas prices went through the roof and house prices went through the floor; we had wars, the Olympics, and delightful scandals like sanctimonious presidential candidate John Edwards' affair and New York's arrogant governor Eliot Spitzer visiting prostitutes. There was just too much this year, and it has made editing our annual book a tough job!

This is book is a history book. Editorial cartoons are a mirror on our society. Cartoonists don't just chronicle events; we reflect the feelings of our readers as they react to events in the world around them. We think our annual Best Political Cartoons of the Year book is the best history book of all. Cartoons might first seem to be shallow and funny, but they are really a thoughtful survey of our culture, our emotions, our spirit, and our times.

We edit this book with no political point of view in mind. We try to show a broad range of perspectives and styles as we cram as much content as we can into our 288 little pages. The cartoonists featured here are the best the profession has to offer, and complete archives of their recent work can be found on our Web site at www.cagle.com, updated every day as new cartoons come in. We would also encourage our readers to visit our cartoon and columnist site at www.caglepost.com, the best commentary site on the Web. To run our cartoons in your publication, Web site, newsletter, or on t-shirts or mugs, visit our store site at www.politicalcartoons.com. Newspapers subscribe to our cartoon package service at www.caglecartoons.com. When you finish our book, visit us for more cartoons online.

... And Another Book!

There was too much going on in 2008 and too many great cartoons about the presidential election. We just couldn't fit it all into this book – so we came out with two books this year!

Our *BIG Book of Campaign 2008 Political Cartoons* is volume two of this *Best Political Cartoons of the Year* book. None of the cartoons in the two books are duplicated, and having a book entirely dedicated to the marathon presidential campaign allowed us to better cover the issues that consumed us in this news-packed year.

We have 3:00 a.m. phone calls, Hillary and Bill Clinton, Sarah Palin, Obama's crazy preacher Jeremiah Wright, mudslinging, conventions, Oprah Winfrey, McCain's countless houses, the crowd of candidates in the primaries – all topics that dominated the news, but we couldn't find enough space in this book.

Every true cartoon wonk will have to have both books, or history will be incomplete.

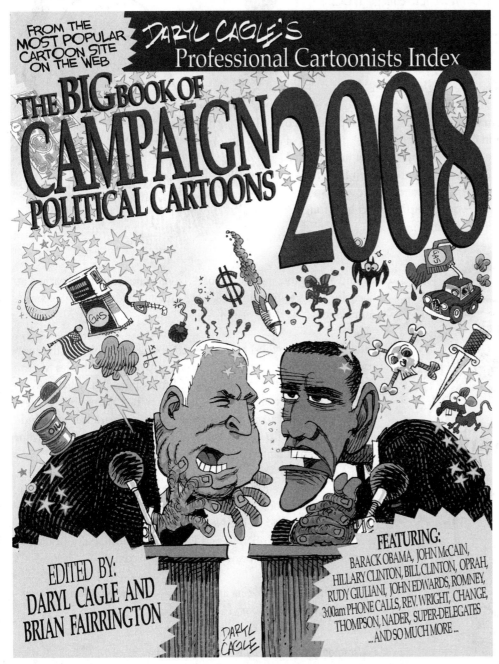

FROM THE MOST POPULAR CARTOON SITE ON THE WEB

DARYL CAGLE'S Professional Cartoonists Index

THE BIG BOOK OF CAMPAIGN 2008 POLITICAL CARTOONS

EDITED BY: DARYL CAGLE AND BRIAN FAIRRINGTON

FEATURING:
BARACK OBAMA, JOHN McCAIN, HILLARY CLINTON, BILL CLINTON, OPRAH, RUDY GIULIANI, JOHN EDWARDS, ROMNEY, 3:00am PHONE CALLS, REV. WRIGHT, CHANGE, THOMPSON, NADER, SUPER-DELEGATES ...AND SO MUCH MORE...

About the Editor-Cartoonists

Daryl Cagle is the daily editorial cartoonist for MSNBC.com. Daryl's editorial cartoon site with MSNBC.com (www.cagle.com) is the most popular cartoon website of any kind on the Internet. It is also the most widely used education site in social studies classrooms around the world.

For the past 30 years, Daryl has been one of America's most prolific cartoonists. Raised in California, Daryl went to college at UC Santa Barbara and then moved to New York City, where he worked for 10 years with Jim Henson's Muppets, illustrating scores of books, magazines, calendars, and all manner of products.

In 2001, Daryl started a new syndicate, Cagle Cartoons, Inc. (www.caglecartoons.com), which distributes the cartoons of sixty editorial cartoonists and columnists to more than 800 newspapers in the United States, Canada, and Latin America. Daryl is a past president of the National Cartoonists Society and current president of the National Cartoonists Society Foundation. He is a frequent guest on Fox News, CNN and MSNBC. Daryl is a popular and entertaining public speaker. Interested in having Daryl speak to your group? Contact us through www.caglecartoons.com for more information.

Brian Fairrington, a graduate of Arizona State University, earned a bachelor's degree in political science and a master's degree in communications.

Brian is one of the most accomplished young cartoonists in the country. Brian was the recipient of the Locher Award, the Charles M. Schulz Award, and several Society of Professional Journalists awards and Gold Circle Awards. He is a regular on the Phoenix-based television talk show Horizon, for which one of his appearances garnered an Emmy award. Brian has also been a guest on Imus inthe Morning and was recently featured on CBS News Sunday Morning.

Brian's cartoons are nationally syndicated to more than 800 newspapers and publications in America with Caglecartoons.com. His cartoons have appeared in The New York Times, USA Today, and Time, as well as on CNN, MSNBC, and Fox News. Additionally, his cartoons regularly appear on www.cagle.msnbc.com.

Brian is a native of Arizona and is married to the wonderful Stacey Heywood; they have four children.

Fairrington and Cagle, by Brian Fairrington

We Want to Hear From You

As the reader of this book, you are our most important critic and commentator. We Value your opinion and want to know what we're doing right, what we could do better, what areas you'd like to see us publish in, and any other words of wisdom you're willing to pass our way.

As an associate publisher for Que Publishing, I welcome your comments. You can email or write me directly to let me know what you did or didn't like about this book– as wells as what we can do to make our books better.

When you write, please be sure to include this book's title, *The Best Political Cartoons of the Year, 2009 Edition,* and editor/cartoonists, Daryl Cagle and Brian Fairrington, as well as your name, email address and phone number. I will carefully review your comments and share them with the editors of this book.

Email:
feedback@quepublishing.com
Mail: Greg Weigand
Associate Publisher
Que Publishing
800 East 96th Street
Indianapolis, IN 46240 USA

ANGEL BOLIGAN, El Universal, Mexico

Not So Funny in China

China hosted the Olympics in 2008 and news from China was in the headlines all year long, with a massive earthquake in Szechwan province, Olympic torch relay protests against Chinese rule in Tibet, and a scandal about milk tainted with industrial melamine.

I went on a speaking tour in China as part of a cultural exchange through the U.S. State Department, talking to college audiences about my political cartoons and what it's like to be an editorial cartoonist in America. I was there just before the Olympics, at the time of the earthquake. I had an opportunity to meet with lots of Chinese cartoonists, to learn about the cartooning profession there, and to meet lots of eager, interesting college audiences.

The best measures of political freedom in any country are their political cartoons and whether cartoonists are allowed to draw their own leaders. Chinese cartoonists almost never draw their leaders, and my Bush-bashing cartoons were very foreign to Chinese audiences, who seemed genuinely concerned for my safety; they thought I was in danger from the politicians I lampooned in America. The questions were the same, wherever I went:

Q: Do your cartoons hurt your personal relationships with the politicians you draw?
A: No, I don't have personal relationships with the people I draw.

Q: Do you worry that your drawings will hurt the reputation of someone you have drawn?
A: No, if one of my cartoons hurts the reputation of a politician that I am criticizing, then I am pleased. (Sometimes the crowd murmurs when I say this. It doesn't seem to be what they expect me to say.)

Q: Do you ever apologize for your cartoons?
A: Sometimes, but only if I make an error or if the cartoon is misunderstood. Usually the people who are angry about a cartoon are the people I intend to make angry, and I am happy to make them angry. (The crowd murmurs at this answer, too.)

Q: Do you ever draw cartoons that are supportive of China?
A: No, I don't draw cartoons that support anything. I just criticize. In America we have a special term for positive, supportive cartoons, we call them: "greeting cards."

On one stop in China I gave a speech to a college class at an American Consulate and, unlike my other speeches in China, I showed some cartoons about China. At the time of my visit, Chinese passions were running high against worldwide protests of the Olympic torch relay, protesting China's rule of Tibet. I showed a series of cartoons criticizing China with the Olympic logo, from countries around the world. The audience gasped in horror, having never seen anything like these cartoons – then they laughed; after all, these are just cartoons. Here they are, below and on the next pages.

RAINER HACHFELD
Germany

DENG COY MIEL
Thailand

Q: *Now that you have visited China, and have learned more about China, will you be drawing cartoons that support China?*
A: Probably not.

The students asked whether I was excited about the Olympics (no, I wasn't) and what I thought about the earthquake (it was terrible, but I wish President Bush had responded to Hurricane Katrina as quickly as the Chinese government responded to the earthquake).

I learned what the Chinese think are funny — pigs and homosexuals. If I ever give a speech in China again, I'll be sure to show all of my cartoons that feature pigs and homo-sexuals.

On all but one occasion, I didn't show cartoons about China. I just wanted to show how I draw disrespectful cartoons about American leaders. That was enough to shock these audi-ences and show how different our press freedoms are. I was always asked how China is depicted in cartoons, and I answered that there are four symbols of China in internation-al editorial cartoons: a panda bear, a Chinese dragon, the Great Wall, or the guy standing in front of the tank in Tiananmen Square — the

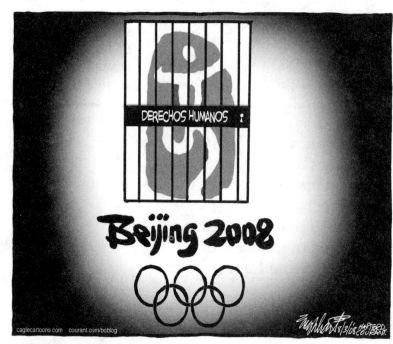

BOB ENGLEHART, The Hartford Courant

THOMAS "TAB" BOLDT, The Calgary Sun, Canada

audience gasps — many of the students have never seen the famous photo, and the subject of the Tiananmen Square "incident" is rarely discussed. At one speech, I mentioned the four symbols, the audience gasped, and one student jumped up, saying, "Oh! Oh! What kind of dragon?!"

I explained to the college kids about "censorship" in America, and that the government never censors cartoonists, but that freedom of the press belongs to the guy who owns the press and cartoonists often complain about their editors. This seemed to be a difficult distinction for them to grasp, in a country where the government owns or controls the press.

The Chinese have embraced capitalism; the country is booming, but the Chinese are eager to prove that economic freedom and political freedom are separate matters that don't go together. The willingness of the Chinese to accept the restrictions on their press is shocking to my American sensibilities — just as my cartoons were shocking to the Chinese.

– Daryl Cagle

PATRICK CHAPPATTE
International Herald Tribune

PETER LEWIS, Australia

BOB GORRELL

Grim Days for Editorial Cartooning

2008 was another terrible year for the business of editorial cartooning. The decline of newspapers continued to take a toll on the profession as more cartoonists than ever lost their jobs. Newspapers who lost cartoonists didn't refill the positions and cartoonists seemed to be at the top of the cost-cutting list as declines in readership and advertising revenue pummeled the newspaper industry.

Newsrooms across the country have suffered massive cutbacks and it may be that editorial cartoonists are losing their jobs in proportion with other journalists; but since the ranks of employed cartoonists are so small (generally estimated at less than 100 jobs) the cuts seem more dramatic.

The decline in the editorial cartooning business happens at the same time that editorial cartoons are more popular than ever. Cartoonists enjoy a huge audience on the Internet, and the audience for our Cartoonist Index web site (www.cagle.com) continues to grow. Kids who spend all day surfing the web don't read newspapers; the shrinking readership of newspapers is becoming more elderly. Social Studies teachers around the world use editorial cartons in their classrooms, and are required to teach editorial cartoons for state mandated testing, but the teachers and students use sites like www.cagle.com where they can see hundreds of political cartoons, rather then the local newspaper, where they will probably find only one on any given day.

With only a handful of exceptions, cartoonists don't get jobs working for web sites in the same way as they did working for newspapers. Web sites don't subscribe to syndicated cartoonists like newspapers do, so the income of cartoonists is quickly being choked off. Ironically, this is all happening at the same time that cartoonists are doing their best work ever, for a huge audience of fans, and at a time when a troubled world needs political cartoonists more than ever.

Newspapers are putting more resources into their web sites as they see their readership turn to the web, but advertising on the web doesn't bring in the income that supported newspapers in the past. Also,

Here is a partial list of cartoonists who lost full time jobs or who retired during the last year.

Jim Borgman, The Cincinatti Enquirer (OH). Buy out.

Eric Devericks, The Seattle Times. Laid off.

Lee Judge, The Kansas City Star. Laid off.

Don Wright, The Palm Beach Post (FL). Buy out.

Steve Greenberg, The Venture County Star (CA). Laid off.

Stuart Carlson, The Milwaukee Journal-Sentinel (WI). Buy out.

Dwane Powell, The News & Observer (Raleigh, NC). Voluntarily left instead of taking part-time status.

Jim Lange, The Oklahoman (Oklahoma City, OK). "Early" retirement.

Chip Bok, The Akron Beacon-Journal (OH). Buy Out.

Peter Dunlap-Shohl, The Anchorage Daily News (AK). Buy out.

Sandy Huffaker, retired from syndication.

M.e. Cohen, freelance, Retired from editorial cartooning, still illustrating.

Jake Fuller, Gainesville Sun (FL). Laid off.

Dave Granlund, MetroWest Daily News (Framingham, MA). Laid Off.

Paul Combs, left syndication after leaving the Tampa Tribune (FL).

Mike Shelton, The Orange County Register (CA). Laid off.

Gordon Campbell, Inland Valley Daily Bulletin (Ontario, CA). Laid off.

Richard Crowson, Wichita Eagle (KS). Laid off.

Mike Peters, Dayton Daily News (OH), Cut back on the number of editorial cartoons he draws.

Dick Adair, The Honolulu Advertiser (HI). Laid Off.

Ann Telnaes, quit print syndication to focus on animation.

David Catrow, Springfield News-Sun (OH). Left to work on other projects.

newspaper web sites don't have a presence that demands a large audience. The top news sites, like Yahoo! News, MSNBC.com, CNN.com, and Google News all have huge partner sites that drive traffic to them. A typical newspaper site has no reason to exist on the web, and is usually dwarfed by the audience of the local television stations' news sites.

Some cartoonists are following newspapers down the same web hole, thinking that the future of editorial cartoons is web animation. Although animated editorial cartoons on the Web can be popular and creatively successful, there is an attitude on the web that content should be free and it is rare that a cartoonist can find a paying client for animation on the web. Some cartoonists are working crazy hours, doing blogs and animations for their newspapers' failing web sites, in an effort to keep their jobs in print.

Even as the business declines, we're not seeing fewer cartoons. As editorial cartoonists lose their jobs, many of them continue drawing cartoons on a freelance basis, for less money, as a hobby in retirement or a second job. We continue to get flooded with queries from new cartoonists who want to get into the "business" of editorial cartooning. It appears that there will be no shortage of political cartoons, even if all the cartoonists lose their newspaper jobs.

My grim prediction for our cartooning profession is the same as for journalists in general: As we all lose our jobs, we all become freelance bloggers, writing and drawing for a huge audience, on our own, in the evening – after we get home from our real jobs.   – *Daryl Cagle*

Cam Cardow, Ottawa Citizen

Pulitzer Prize: Michael Ramirez

Michael Ramirez of the conservative Investors Business Daily won the Pulitzer Prize in 2008 for this portfolio of twenty cartoons from 2007. It is the second Pulitzer Prize for Michael, who also won in 1994 when he worked for the Memphis Commercial Appeal.

It is interesting that the award comes at this time because Michael was recently laid off from his job as cartoonist for the Los Angeles Times, which now has no editorial cartoonist. The Tribune Company owns The LA Times, The Baltimore Sun, and The Chicago Tribune, all newspapers with a rich tradition of editorial cartooning that no longer employ an editorial cartoonist.

Our congratulations go out to our friend, Michael and to the Investors Business Daily for this well deserved honor. Michael has a new book, "Everyone has the Right to My Opinion," that is coming out at the same time as our "Best Political Cartoons of the Year" book. Michael has given us some excerpts from the introductions to his book to share here with his winning cartoons.

I'm an editorial cartoonist. I'm not a writer. If I could write I would be a columnist.

My publisher wanted me to recount stories like the time I won my first Pulitzer and I was greeted at the award ceremony at Columbia University by an enormous protest. Several protestors approached our car. I realized they had no idea what I looked like when they handed me a flyer protesting myself. So I joined the picket line. I may be the only Pulitzer Prize winner who has protested himself.

Or the time I was investigated by the Secret Service over one of my cartoons.

Or the time I was in Havana interviewing the Minister of Information. He refused to answer questions about imprisoned journalists, censorship, the Brothers in Arms flight that was shot down in international airspace,

MICHAEL RAMIREZ
by Michael Ramirez

or the tugboat full of Cuban refugees that was capsized outside of Havana Harbor drowning most of its occupants.

I brought up the elaborate political process Cuban journalists had to go through to get into print. I brought up the fact that Cuban editorial cartoonists could not draw cartoons of Fidel or Che Guevara. I told him in the United States we believe a country that cannot make fun of its leaders is usually a country imprisoned by its leaders. I asked him one last question, the camera zooming in on his face, "What is your favorite Fidel Castro joke?" His face went ashen. He was speechless. And I got my answer.

It was the same answer William M. Tweed and Tammany Hall gave 120 years earlier in reaction to Thomas Nast's cartoons. Boss Tweed was a little more vociferous in his condemnation, "Stop them damn pictures. I don't care so much what the papers say about me. My constituents don't know how to read, but they can't help seeing them damned pictures!" It was clear the Castro regime recognized the power of the pen.

… Editorial cartoons are a check to the erosion of our liberties and a first line of defense to the advance of the unrestrained power of government. One good editorial cartoon can have a significant impact on the political dialogue of the day. If done well, it can influence those who govern to govern responsibly, and expose them when they do not.

Einstein once said, "Two things are infinite: the universe and human stupidity; and I'm not sure about the universe." Einstein was right. It is this axiom which makes political cartooning important. The peo-

ple who ultimately govern will make mistakes. They are human after all. But history has demonstrated that power can turn leaders into monsters. Editorial cartoonists will gladly point out the shortcomings of the powerful in an effort to keep them human.

And while it is quite remarkable that cartoons can have such an impact, it is equally remarkable and short-sighted that newspapers, in their infinite wisdom, are relin-

quishing this influence and abandoning the position of editorial cartoonist. H.L. Mencken, once said, "Give me a good cartoonist and I can throw out half the editorial staff." Poll after poll has demonstrated, of the people who read the editorial page, the editorial cartoon continues to be the most popular feature on the page.

Part of the damage is self-inflicted. Where the modern trend in editorial cartooning has been to make simple jokes about current affairs, humor without a substantive statement diminishes the importance of the editorial cartoon. Editorial cartoonists who don't take their jobs seriously should not expect to be taken seriously.

An editorial cartoon is not just a "funny picture." An editorial cartoon is a fine instrument of journalism. At times, it is sharp and refined, its message cutting quickly to the point, at times blunt, with its dark imagery seizing the readers' attention.

As with any editorial, the cartoon has a point. It tells a story. It defines an issue. It challenges hypocrisy. It reveals the best and the worst of humanity. It calls the reader to arms against the complacent, the lethargic, the evildoers, the indolent body politic, and the champions of the status quo. It exposes the assorted predators of society.

An editorial cartoon is not humorous for the sake of humor. It is not controversial for the sake of controversy. It is neither conservative nor liberal. Whether you agree with it philosophically or not, a good editorial cartoon engages the reader in debate. It informs and challenges. It draws the reader into the democratic process.

– Michael Ramirez

THE GREAT WALL

I should add that I was with Michael in Havana when he asked the Cuban Minister for his favorite Castro joke. After going silent and ashen, as Michael describes, the Minister told us that there were no Castro jokes, because Cubans wouldn't think jokes about Castro were funny. When we went back to our hotel, Michael drew a lovely cover on his blank sketchbook with the title "Fidel Castro Joke Book." Of course, the joke was that the all the pages in the "Fidel Castro Joke Book" were blank. We went back and Michael presented the book as a gift to the Minister, who didn't think it was very funny.

I thought it was funny.

–Daryl Cagle

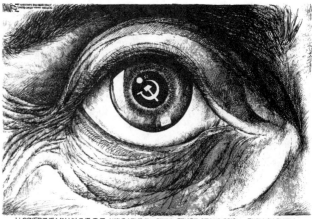

THE ANCHOR

POL POT HAT
2 MILLION DEATHS

KIM JONG-IL
SUNGLASSES
2 MILLION STARVED

MAO T-SHIRT
OVER 60 MILLION
DEATHS

USSR SCARF
OVER 40 MILLION
DEATHS

CHE T-SHIRT
400 EXECUTIONS
LA CABAÑA

CASTRO
FATIGUES
110,000 DEATHS

MAO BAG
SHINING PATH
70,000 DEATHS

FASHIONS FOR THE IGNORANT CELEBRITY

THE GLOBAL WAR
ON TERROR
IS JUST A
BUMPER STICKER

LONDON

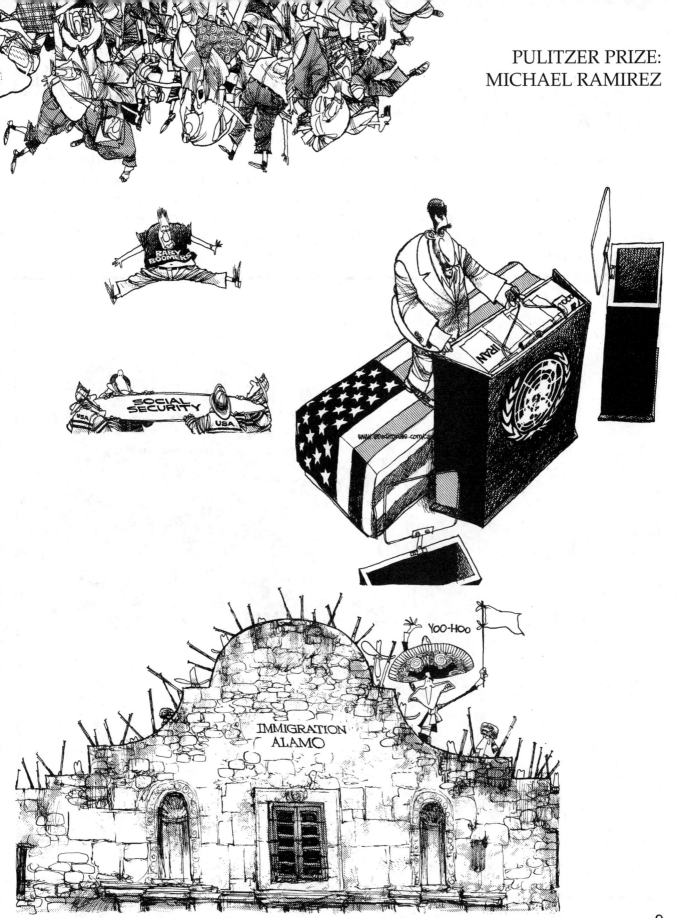

Hollywood Writers Strike

Hollywood screenwriters went on strike this year against their production companies. At first the screenwriters had a sympathetic cause – wanting royalties on the digital usage of their work – plus they were the David to the producers' Goliath. It was difficult to ignore that the TV writers were, by far, the highest paid writers of any kind. As the strike dragged on and after America missed a season of their favorite shows, most people – including cartoonists – were fed up with the writers.

DWAYNE BOOTH
Mr. Fish

BILL DAY, Memphis Commercial Appeal

HENRY PAYNE
Detroit News

CARTOONISTS IN SOLIDARITY WITH THE WRITERS STRIKE

R.J. MATSON, New York Observer

MIKE KEEFE
Denver Post

HOLLYWOOD WRITERS STRIKE

"LOOKS LIKE THE WRITERS' STRIKE IS ON..."
BILL SCHORR

"HOLLYWOOD WRITERS ON STRIKE."
HENRY PAYNE, Detroit News

WHEN THOSE WRITERS GO ON STRIKE, THEY GO ON STRIKE!

PICKET LINE

JOHN DARKOW, Columbia Daily Tribune (MO)

HOLLYWOOD

WRITER'S STRIKE

BOB ENGLEHART, Hartford Courant

HOLLYWOOD STARS CAMPAIGN FOR THEIR FAVORITE PRESIDENTIAL CANDIDATES...

I SEE THERE'S A GOOD SIDE TO THIS "WRITERS' STRIKE"

JERRY HOLBERT, Boston Herald

AS AN ACTRESS, HOW DO YOU FEEL ABOUT THE SCREEN WRITERS' STRIKE?

DANA SUMMERS, Orlando Sentinel

PATRICK O'CONNOR, Los Angeles Daily News

GARY MCCOY, Cagle Cartoons

PATRICK CHAPPATTE
International Herald Tribune

MIKE THOMPSON
Detroit Free Press

NIK SCOTT
Australia

15

Murder of Bhutto

Former Prime Minister of Pakistan Benazir Bhutto had brought hope to many in the country when she returned after nine years of self-imposed exile to run again for political office. Bhutto was widely disliked, having been forced out of the country on charges of corruption, and she knew she was in constant danger. Still, it came as something of a shock when she was assassinated in a haze of gunfire during a political rally. News of Bhutto's death sparked riots across Pakistan, even as President Pervez Musharraf condemned the tragedy. Bhutto had been a strong U.S. ally, and many cartoonists mourned her death, though some were still skeptical of her politics.

ARES
Cuba

caglecartoons.com/espanol

STEVE GREENBERG, Ventura County Star

DEMOCRACY IN PAKISTAN

VOTE FOR ONE

BENAZIR BHUTTO
FORMER PRIME MINISTER

PERVEZ MUSHARRAF
PRESIDENT

NAWAZ SHARIF
FORMER PRIME MINISTER

EXTREMISM

SETBACKISTAN

ADAM ZYGLIS
Buffalo News

BALLOT BOX OF A PAKISTANI "DEMOCRACY"

VOTE BHUTTO

PAKISTAN EARLY VOTING

PARLIAMENTARY ELECTIONS

BHUTTO

JOHN TREVER, Albuquerque Journal

BENAZIR BHUTTO 1953-2007

MUSHARRAF

BITCH.

DARYL CAGLE, MSNBC.com

1953 — BENAZIR BHUTTO — 2007

MILT PRIGGEE, Politicalcartoons.com

DEMOCRACY'S FALLEN STAR
CAL GRONDAHL, Utah Standard Examiner

17

NATE BEELER
Washington Examiner

HENRY PAYNE
Detroit News

A SECOND TIGER ATTACK...

MARSHALL RAMSEY
Clarion Ledger (MI)

MIKE LUCKOVICH
The Atlanta Journal-Constitution

NOW WHERE IS THAT CAT?...

TIGER ENCLOSURE

PAKISTAN

PAKISTANI TIGER ATTACK

JEFF KOTERBA
Omaha World Herald

MICHAEL RAMIREZ
Investors Business Daily

www.IBDeditorials.com/cartoons

Clemens Faces Congress

Major League pitcher Roger Clemens never took the mound in 2008, but that's not to say he didn't make any career-defining appearances. In February, Clemens took the stand before a Congressional committee to address allegations he took performance-enhancing drugs, leading many in the media to ask whether Congress didn't have better things to do anyhow. Fallout included an FBI investigation into whether Clemens lied under oath, further tarnishing the pitcher's image in the eyes of fans (and cartoonists).

DON WRIGHT, Palm Beach Post

To Jimmy-Roger Clemens

HORMONE INJECTIONS AREN'T ALWAYS NECESSARY FOR HUMAN GROWTH

STEVE BREEN
San Diego Union Tribune

REX BABIN
Sacramento Bee

DON WRIGHT
Palm Beach Post

"...A SIMPLE "NO" WILL SUFFICE, MR. CLEMENS..."

WALT HANDELSMAN
Newsday

CLEMENS FACES CONGRESS

DICK LOCHER, Chicago Tribune

JEFF STAHLER, Columbus Dispatch

MIKE LUCKOVICH, The Atlanta Journal-Constitution

JACK OHMAN
Portland Oregonian

DANA SUMMERS, Orlando Sentinel

23

Mitchell Report

Visions of asterisks danced in the heads of cartoonists when former Sen. George Mitchell released his brutal 409-page report on the prevalence of anabolic steroids and human growth hormone in Major League Baseball. The investigation found plenty of big names to blame, detailing 89 players, including stars Barry Bonds, Roger Clemens, and Andy Pettitte, as alleged users and castigated baseball executives for turning a blind eye to the abuses. Cartoonists compiled their own lists of the naughty.

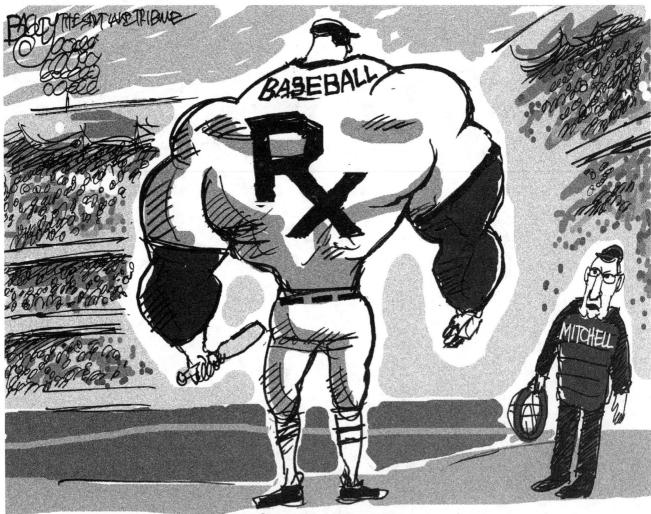

"TIME TO RETIRE THE JERSEY."

PAT BAGLEY, Salt Lake Tribune (UT)

STRONG ENOUGH TO TEAR A RECORDS BOOK IN HALF!!

MIKE LANE
Cagle Cartoons

ROBERT ARIAIL
The State, SC

DARYL CAGLE
MSNBC.COM

25

26

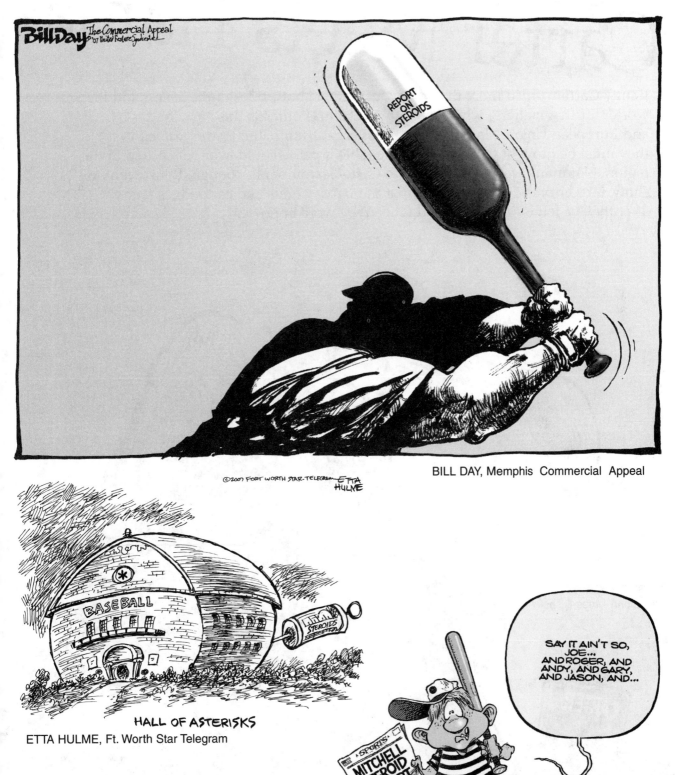

BILL DAY, Memphis Commercial Appeal

HALL OF ASTERISKS

ETTA HULME, Ft. Worth Star Telegram

BOB GORRELL
Creators Syndicate

Carter Meets Hamas

Jimmy Carter ruffled more than a few feathers on both sides of the aisle — and the world, for that matter – when he met with Hamas officials this year. To the U.S. and European Union, Hamas is a terrorist organization, but Carter argued that they must be brought to the negotiating table if peace could ever be reached in the region. Not many were sympathetic to Carter's arguments, though. It just went to show, former presidents can make just as many citizens and cartoonists angry after they've left office as they did when they were in power.

GARY BROOKINS
Richmond Times-Dispatch

"WHY, IT HAS SOFT, FLUFFY FEATHERS...IT MUST BE A DOVE!"

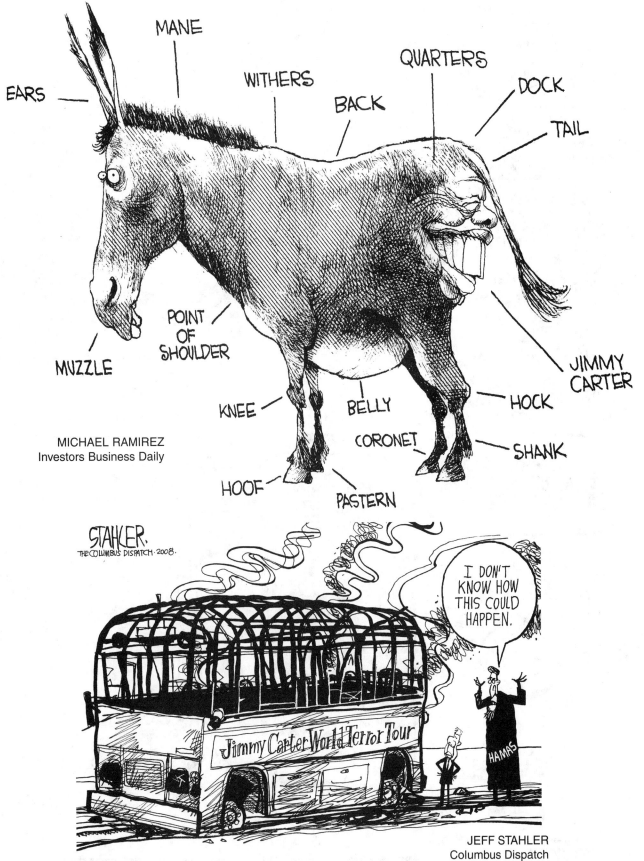

EARS

MANE

WITHERS

QUARTERS

DOCK

BACK

TAIL

POINT
OF
SHOULDER

MUZZLE

JIMMY
CARTER

MICHAEL RAMIREZ
Investors Business Daily

KNEE

BELLY

HOCK

CORONET

SHANK

HOOF

PASTERN

STAHLER.
THE COLUMBUS DISPATCH · 2008.

I DON'T
KNOW HOW
THIS COULD
HAPPEN.

Jimmy Carter World Terror Tour

HAMAS

JEFF STAHLER
Columbus Dispatch

Dry Bones

CARTER'S MISSION?

IT'S OBVIOUS!

OBVIOUS?

CARTER CAME TO ASK THE TERRORISTS TO "COOL IT" UNTIL AFTER OBAMA WINS!

WOW!

THESE DAYS IT'S DIFFICULT TO TELL THE DIFFERENCE BETWEEN COMPLETE PARANOIA . . .

. . . AND ASTUTE POLITICAL ANALYSIS!

DryBonesBlog.com

YAAKOV KIRSCHEN
Jerusalem Post, Israel

32

NATURALLY, THIS WILL BE MISINTERPRETED BY THOSE WHO FAIL TO UNDERSTAND MY PATHETIC DESIRE TO BE A PLAYER.

HAMAS

DEERING
ARKANSAS DEMOCRAT-GAZETTE
©2008 CREATORS SYND. INC.

JOHN DEERING, Arkansas Democrat Gazette

The Washington Examiner
CAGLECARTOONS.COM

HAMAS HAS ASSURED ME THERE CAN BE PEACE IF ISRAEL PLAYS BALL!

JIMMY

HERE'S THE BALL THEY GAVE ME...

NATE BEELER, Washington Examiner

IF JIMMY CARTER COULD TRAVEL IN TIME

JERRY HOLBERT, Boston Herald

ISRAEL REFUSES TO PROTECT JIMMY CARTER

JERRY HOLBERT, Boston Herald

STEVE
SACK
Minneapolis
Star-Tribune

Turmoil in Tibet

Though talks between the exiled Tibetan Dalai Lama and the Chinese government resumed again this year (with little progress made), the issue got more attention than it had in some time due to the media frenzy surrounding the Beijing Olympics. Protesters lined the Olympic torch's path around the globe and made appearances at the games, while China made every effort to squash their voices. Cartoonists were mostly sympathetic to the Tibetan plight, nailing China for its human rights abuses.

TIBET

DON WRIGHT
Palm Beach Post

BEIJING OLYMPICS

NATE BEELER
Washington Examiner

DAVID HORSEY, Seattle Post Intelligencer

S. KELLEY THE TIMES-PICAYUNE ©2008

STEVE KELLEY
New Orleans Times-Picayune

"THEY FOUND SOMEONE TO RUN THE OLYMPIC TORCH PAST ALL THE PROTESTERS..."

JOHN SHERFFIUS
Boulder Daily Camera

PETER BROELMAN, Australia

SCOTT STANTIS
Birmingham News

FREE TIBET!

Beijing 2008

BILL SCHORR

WALT HANDELSMAN
Newsday

"...CAREFUL... IF THE PROTESTORS DON'T GET YOU, THE LEAD PAINT ON THE TORCH WILL..."

STEPHANE PERAY
Thailand

STEPHANE PERAY
Thailand

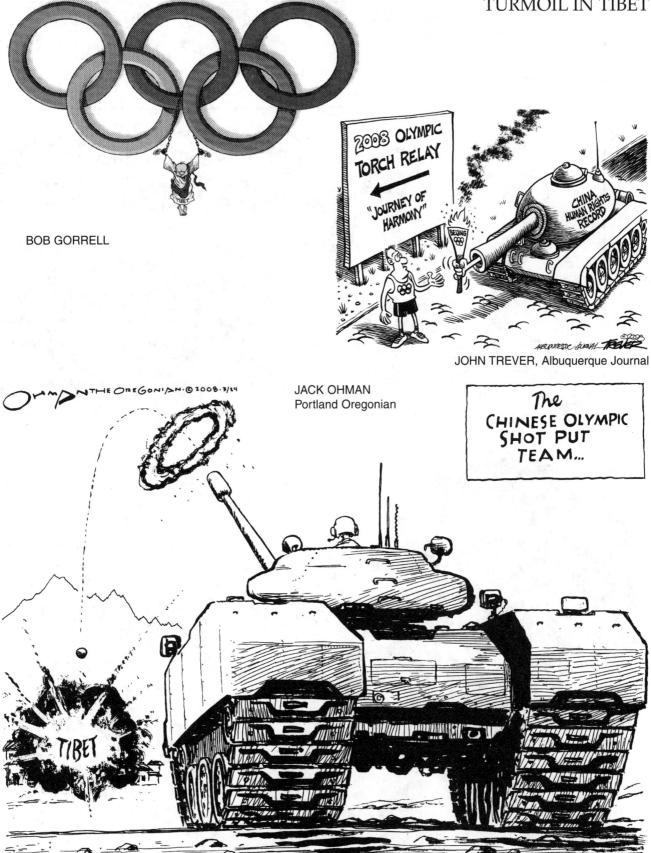

BOB GORRELL

JOHN TREVER, Albuquerque Journal

JACK OHMAN
Portland Oregonian

STEVE BENSON
Arizona Republic

STEVE SACK, Minneapolis Star-Tribune

OSMANI SIMANCA, Brazil

www.caglecartoons.com/espanol   SIMANCA

INGRID RICE
British Columbia
Canada

THE GLOBAL VILLAGE TAKES PART IN THE OLYMPIC TORCH RELAY

MANNY FRANCISCO
Phillippines

YAAKOV KIRSCHEN, Jerusalem Post, Israel

42

CORKY TRINIDAD
Honolulu Star Bulletin

43

Burma Typhoon

The cyclone that hit Myanmar (Burma) on May 3 of this year killed upwards of 100,000 people and caused $10 billion in damage. It was the worst natural disaster in the country's history. But the tragedy was compounded by the unwillingness of the Burmese military junta to allow much foreign aid into the country, leaving nearly one million people homeless and starving. The junta was an easy evil target for cartoonists.

SCOTT STANTIS
Birmingham News

44

JIMMY MARGULIES, The Record (NJ)

IAIN GREEN, Scotland

CHIP BOK, Akron Beacon-Journal

KEEP THOSE BORDERS CLOSED! WE DON'T WANT ANYONE IN THE WAY OF OUR FIRST RESPONDERS!

STEVE SACK
Minneapolis Star-Tribune

DWANE POWELL
Raliegh News & Observer

45

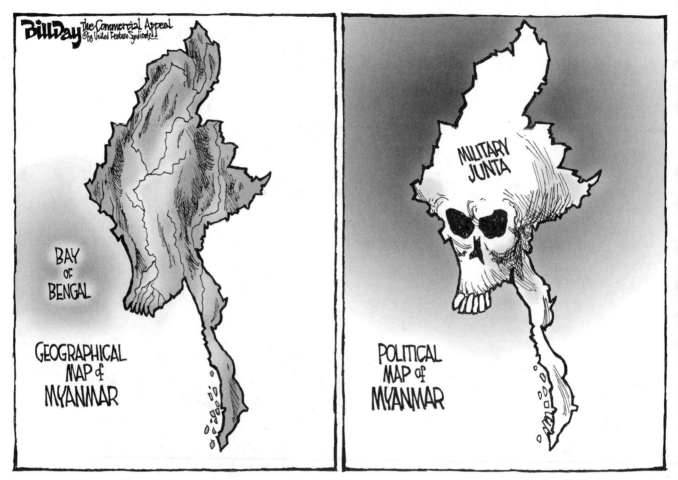

BILL DAY
Memphis Commercial Appeal

PETER LEWIS, Newcastle Herald Australia

INGRID RICE, British Columbia, Canada

MARSHALL RAMSEY, Clarion Ledger (MI)

BURMA TYPHOON

NATE BEELER, Washington Examiner

PAUL ZANETTI, Australia

ROBERT ARIAIL, The State, SC

MANNY FRANCISCO Phillippines

STEVE NEASE, Oakville Beaver (Canada)

CAM CARDOW, Ottawa Citizen

CHRISTO
KOMARNITSKI
Bulgaria

48

BURMA TYPHOON

PATRICK CHAPPATTE, International Herald Tribune

MIKE KEEFE, Denver Post

MICHAEL RAMIREZ
Investors Business Daily

Polar Bears in Peril?

This year the International Union for Conservation of Nature put polar bears on the threatened species list, as their icy habitat quickly melted in rising Arctic Circle temperatures. The melt subjected bears to food shortages and even changes in mating and social patterns. And with "global warming" explicitly listed as their greatest threat, the polar bears became a symbol this year of the growing crisis. This was the year the world's largest land predator was brought down by mankind.

NATE BEELER, Washington Examiner

The Bush administration makes an important emission...

JOHN SHERFFIUS
Boulder Daily Camera

DAVID HORSEY
Seattle Post Intelligencer

ROBERT ARIAIL, The State, SC

BILL DAY, Memphis Commercial Appeal

DENG COY MIEL

MARSHALL RAMSEY, Clarion Ledger (MI)

MIKE LESTER, Rome News-Tribune (GA)

JOHN DARKOW, Columbia Daily Tribune (MO)

POLAR BEARS IN PERIL?

HENRY PAYNE
Detroit News

MIKE LUCKOVICH
The Atlanta Journal-Constitution

Castro Quits!

His enemies had been waiting for this day more than fifty years ... kind of.
Most people thought Fidel Castro wouldn't give up his dictatorship in Cuba until after he'd smoked his last cigar. But the Cuban "president" surprised everyone when, in ailing health, he announced that he'd be handing over control of the country to his brother, Raúl Castro. It was the end of an era, but meant little political change for dysfunctional communist Cuba.

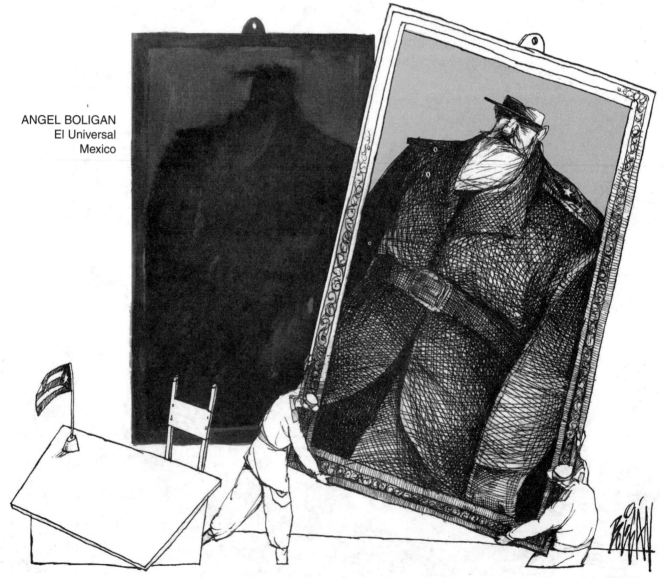

ANGEL BOLIGAN
El Universal
Mexico

DARYL CAGLE
MSNBC.com

DARIO CASTILLEJOS
Diario La Crisis
Mexico

DARIO CASTILLEJOS, Diario La Crisis, Mexico

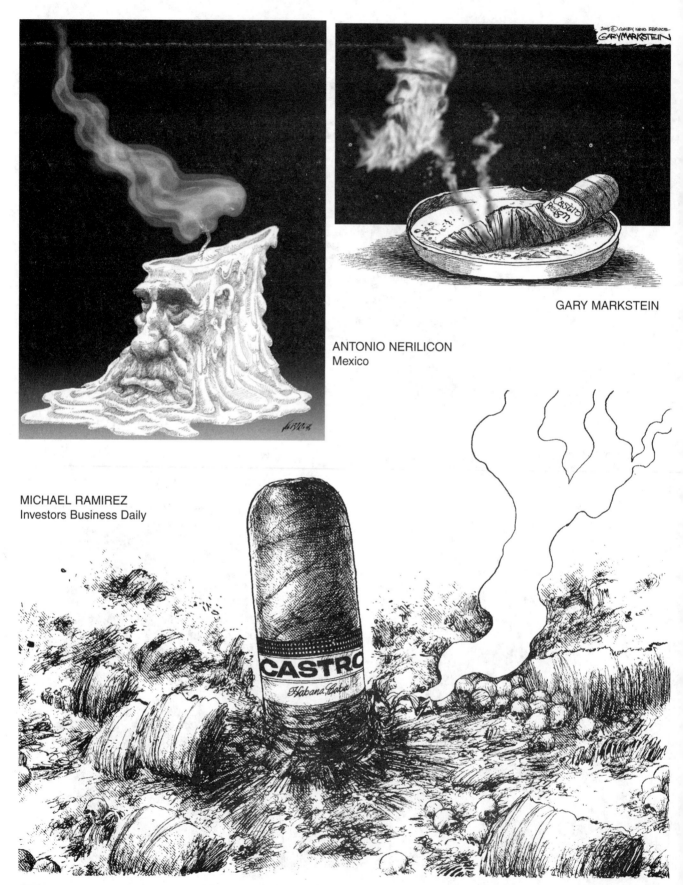

GARY MARKSTEIN

ANTONIO NERILICON
Mexico

MICHAEL RAMIREZ
Investors Business Daily

56

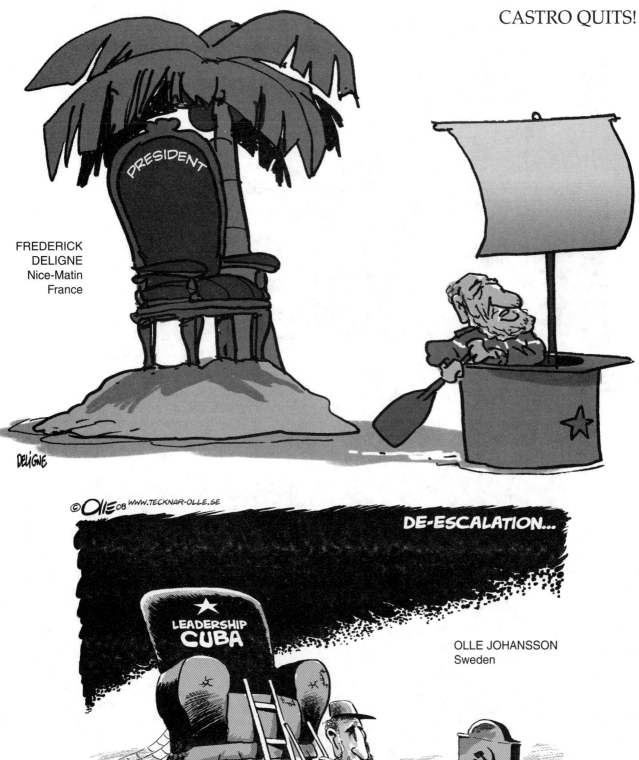

FREDERICK
DELIGNE
Nice-Matin
France

DE-ESCALATION...

OLLE JOHANSSON
Sweden

57

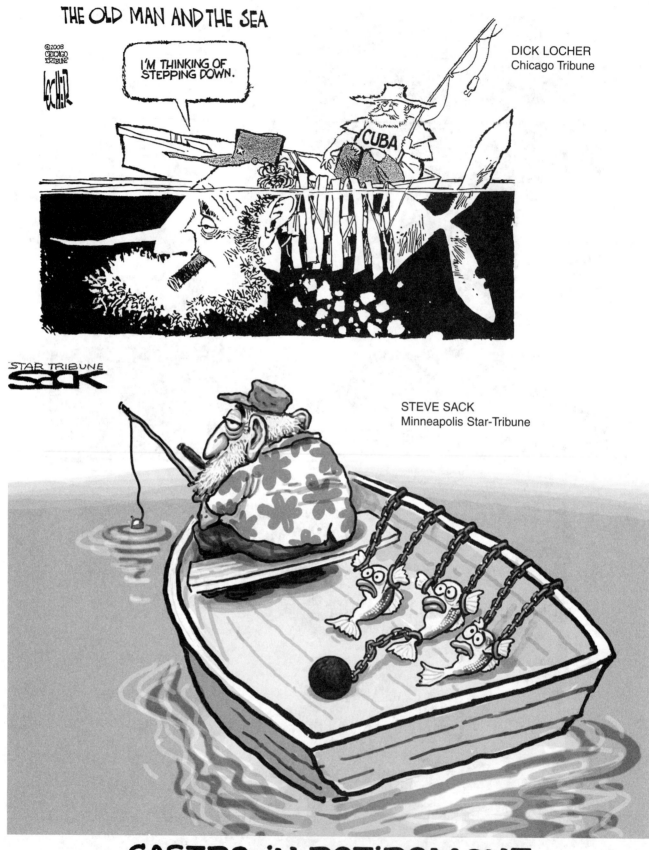

CASTRO IN RETIREMENT

PASSING the TORCH in CUBA...

FIDEL CASTRO

RAUL CASTRO

BILL DAY
Memphis Commercial Appeal

TAYLOR JONES
El Nuevo Dia
Puerto Rico

RIBER HANSSON
Sweden

Politicalcartoons.com

NATE BEELER, Washington Examiner

PATRICK CHAPPATTE
International Herald Tribune

CHRISTO KOMARNITSKI
Bulgaria

TWO RELICS...

DANG IT, FIDEL. WHY CAN'T YOU JUST DIE?!

U.S. CUBA POLICY

DAVID HORSEY
Seattle Post Intelligencer

CASTRO QUITS!

POLICY

PETAR PISMESTROVIC Austria

arcadio/CAGLECARTOONS.com

ARCADIO ESQUIVEL
La Prensa, Panama

"CUBA POSTCASTRO"

ARES, Cuba

61

No Nukes in Iran

After years of tension and mounting pressure from the U.S. and Israel, the International Atomic Energy Agency released a report showing that Iran was indeed developing uranium enrichment for "peaceful purposes" and not to proliferate nuclear weapons. The report was disappointing for the Bush administration but gave cartoonists another opportunity to draw the nasty, unshaven, Iranian President Mahmoud Ahmadinejad.

MATT DAVIES
Journal News, NY

JOHN COLE
Scranton Times-Tribune

ADAM ZYGLIS
Buffalo News

OSMANI SIMANCA
Brazil

63

JACK OHMAN, Portland Oregonian

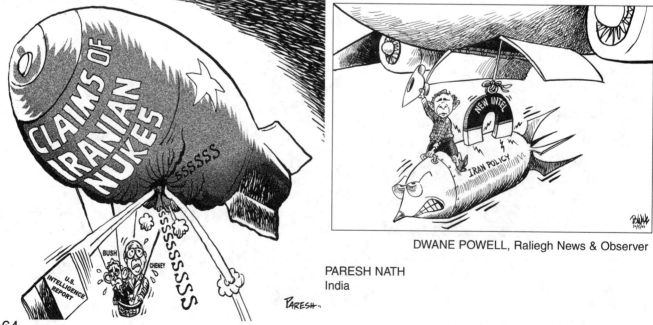

DWANE POWELL, Raliegh News & Observer

PARESH NATH
India

NO NUKES IN IRAN

ROBERT ARIAIL
The State, SC

PAT BAGLEY
Salt Lake Tribune. UT

RICHARD CROWSON
Witchita Eagle

MIKE KEEFE
Denver Post

BILL SCHORR

"PSST, CONDI... WHAT DIDN'T I KNOW, AND WHEN DIDN'T I KNOW IT?"

ARCADIO ESQUIVEL
La Prensa, Panama

CAGLECARTOONS.COM

MIKE LANE
Cagle Cartoons

IRAN DRUM

N.I.E. REPORT

THE MUSEUM OF NUCLEAR THREATS

ETTA HULME, Ft. Worth Star Telegram

"WE'RE NOT REALLY SURE WHAT TO MAKE OF IRAN. NOW IT SEEMS THEY'VE STARTED A NEW PROGRAM MAKING TEDDY BEARS."

GARY BROOKINS, The Richmond Times-Dispatch

JOHN DARKOW, Columbia Daily Tribune (MO)

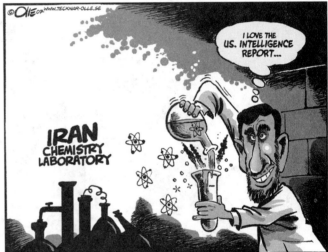

OLLE JOHANSSON, Sweden

STEVE BENSON, Arizona Republic

ED STEIN, Rocky Mountain News

Food Prices!

A bad year of crops and skyrocketing gas prices compounded to raise the cost of nearly all food products nationwide. Americans everywhere felt the pinch at the grocery store–but far, far worse was the plight of those around the globe who fell victim to serious food shortages. As American corporations burned fields of corn for biodiesel, citizens of less fortunate nations starved. Cartoonists in other nations were more generally sensitive to the grand scope of the issue than those stateside, but everyone was concerned.

OSMANI SIMANCA, Brazil

FOOD PRICES

OIL PRICES

RICHARD CROWSON
Witchita Eagle

EXPRESS LANE
$100.⁰⁰ OR LESS

JEFF STAHLER
Columbus Dispatch

69

STEVE NEASE
Oakville Beaver (Canada)

STEVE BREEN
San Diego Union Tribune

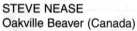

OH.

MATT DAVIES
Journal News, NY

FOOD PRICES!

FOOD PRICES

HYBRID

GARY BROOKINS, The Richmond Times-Dispatch

RICHMOND TIMES-DISPATCH BROOKINS

GRANDMA'S HOUSE

"HEY, WITH THE HIGH COST OF FOOD THESE DAYS, AND GRANNY ON A FIXED INCOME, I JUST DID WHAT I HAD TO DO..."

ED STEIN, Rocky Mountain News

DANA SUMMERS, Orlando Sentinel

BOB ENGLEHART, Hartford Courant

MARSHALL RAMSEY, Clarion Ledger (MI)

JOHN DARKOW, Columbia Daily Tribune (MO)

JEFF PARKER, Florida Today

ROB ROGERS, Pittsburgh Post-Gazette

DICK LOCHER
Chicago Tribune

Killer Tomatoes

There seems to be a food safety scare every year. This time tomatoes were the unlucky culprit. A batch of the juicy veggies was tainted with salmonella farmside before they were shipped off to restaurants. The tomatoes ultimately sickened hundreds of Americans in 23 states. It was one of the country's biggest food-borne illness outbreaks ever, and raised serious questions about the FDA's inspection safety net (or lack thereof). But some cartoonists were just annoyed they couldn't get tomatoes on their sandwiches for a few weeks.

JACK OHMAN, Portland Oregonian

MIKE KEEFE, Denver Post

HENRY PAYNE
Detroit News

ROB ROGERS
Pittsburgh Post-Gazette

PATRICK O'CONNOR, Los Angeles Daily News

KILLER TOMATOES

DREW SHENEMAN, Newark Star Ledger

M.e. COHEN, Politicalcartoons.com

MARSHALL RAMSEY
Clarion Ledger (MI)

MIKE LESTER, Rome News-Tribune (GA)

"I FEEL YOUR PAIN."

Polygamy Problems

Those pesky polygamists made almost as many headlines and cartoons this year as they did underage marriages and babies! A polygamist sect of the Fundamentalist Mormon Church caught the nation's attention this year when Texas authorities raided their compound in Eldorado; they seized 400 children, some of whom were set to marry. The charges fizzled out pretty quickly, and the children were returned to their parents, but the cartoons just kept rolling in.

DAVID FITZSIMMONS, Arizona Daily Star

SORRY. A LITTLE BOY FROM THE POLYGAMIST'S COMPOUND DOWN THE STREET CAME IN AND COMPLETELY CLEANED US OUT.

"Yep, she's grown enough."

CAL GRONDAHL
Utah Standard
Examiner

LOOK, BARBIE, BARBIE, BARBIE, BARBIE, BARBIE, BARBIE, BARBIE, BARBIE, AND ONLY ONE KEN.

...AND YOU ASK WHY I'M DRESSED LIKE THIS.

DARYL CAGLE
MSNBC.COM

BRIAN FAIRRINGTON
Cagle Cartoons

ROBERT ARIAIL
The State, SC

BOB ENGLEHART
Hartford Courant

BILL SCHORR

80

5 Years in Iraq

Two grim milestones were reached in Iraq, five years of war and four thousand U.S. soldiers killed. After getting the same news from Iraq for so long, cartoonists drew far fewer cartoons about the subject this year. Casualties declined, taking Iraq out of the headlines on most days.

ED STEIN
Rocky Mountain News

ADAM ZYGLIS
Buffalo News

ED STEIN
Rocky Mountain News

JEFF PARKER, Florida Today

MATT DAVIES
Journal News, NY

ED STEIN
Rocky Mountain News

FIVE YEARS IN IRAQ

DAVID HORSEY
Seattle Post Intelligencer

BILL DAY
Memphis Commercial Appeal

85

THOMAS "TAB" BOLDT
Calgary Sun (Canada)

LARRY WRIGHT
Detroit News

BRIAN
FAIRRINGTON
Cagle Cartoons

PATRICK O'CONNOR
Los Angeles Daily News

DON WRIGHT
Palm Beach Post

ROB ROGERS, Pittsburgh Post-Gazette

SCOTT STANTIS Birmingham News, AL

IRAQ MATH

FIVE YEARS IN IRAQ

THE PRICE OF SMUGNESS

STEVE GREENBERG
Ventura County Star

PETAR PISMESTROVIC, Austria

SCOTT STANTIS, Birmingham News

High Gas Prices

Gas prices, gas prices, gas prices! It sometimes seemed it was all anyone could think, talk, write, or draw for a few tense months in 2008 – and for good reason. The cost of crude oil topped an all time high of $160 per gallon. When gas prices leveled off above $4 per gallon, Americans felt the sting in their pocket books, and SUV sales tanked, bringing down the American auto industry. When the stock market crashed, oil prices crashed too and prices at the pump tumbled, but the auto industry was still a wreck.

DARYL CAGLE
MSNBC.COM

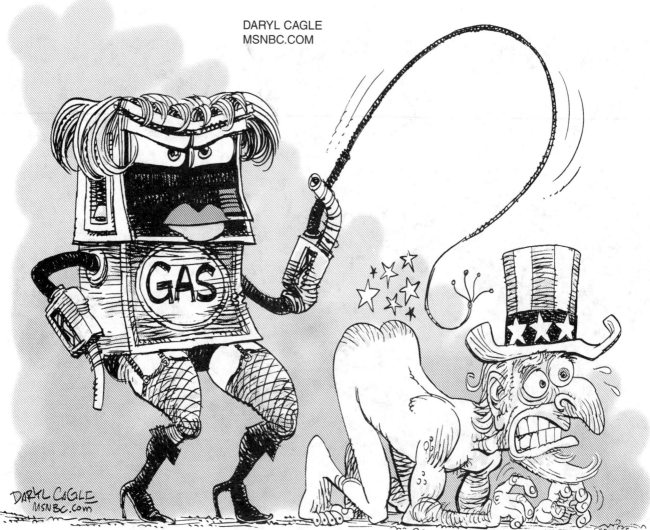

BALL AND CHAIN

MIKE KEEFE
Denver Post

DARYL CAGLE
MSNBC.COM

ADAM ZYGLIS
Buffalo News

GARY VARVEL, Indianapolis Star

DICK LOCHER
Chicago Tribune

JIANPING FAN
China

WAYNE STAYSKAL

GARY MARKSTEIN

WALT HANDELSMAN, Newsday

BILL DAY
Memphis
Commercial Appeal

THOMAS "TAB" BOLDT
Calgary Sun (Canada)

MICHAEL RAMIREZ
Investors Business Daily

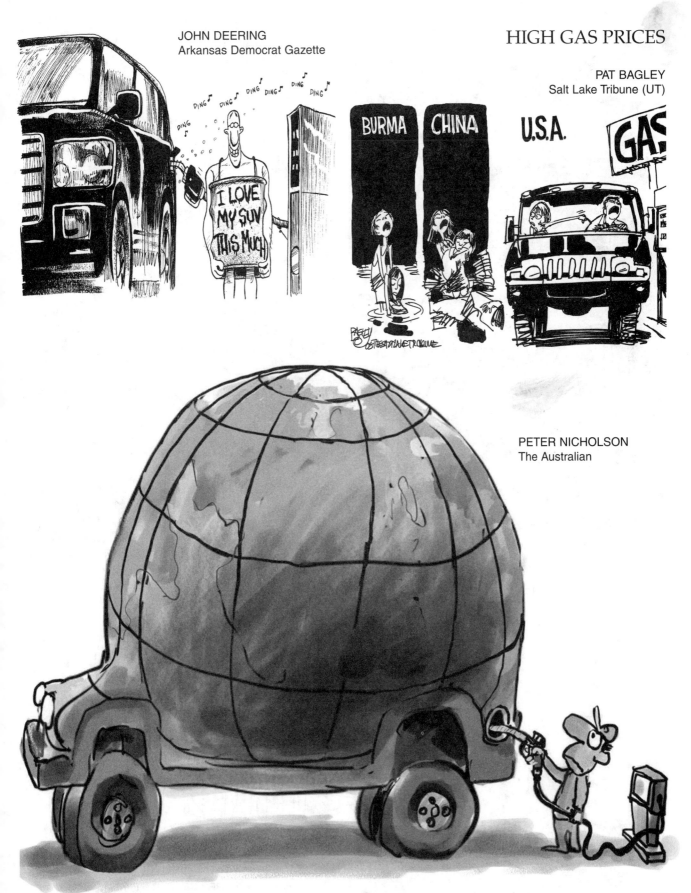

JOHN DEERING
Arkansas Democrat Gazette

HIGH GAS PRICES

PAT BAGLEY
Salt Lake Tribune (UT)

PETER NICHOLSON
The Australian

95

MIKE LUCKOVICH, The Atlanta Journal-Constitution

MIKE LANE, Cagle Cartoons

JOHN TREVER, Albuquerque Journal

JOHN DARKOW, Columbia Daily Tribune (MO)

LARRY WRIGHT, Detroit News

STEVE NEASE, Oakville Beaver (Canada)

PAVEL CONSTANTIN, Romania

BRIAN FAIRRINGTON
Cagle Cartoons

MILT PRIGGEE, Washington CEO

STEVE BENSON
Arizona Republic

SCOTT STANTIS
Birmingham News

DARYL CAGLE
MSNBC.COM

MONTE WOLVERTON, Cagle Cartoons

99

JOHN TREVER, Albuquerque Journal

BOB ENGLEHART, Hartford Courant

STEVE BENSON, Arizona Republic

LARRY WRIGHT, Detroit News

JOE HELLER
Green Bay
Press Gazette

CAL GRONDAHL
Utah Standard Examiner

"$4 per gallon, wow, I didn't know that."

STEVE BENSON
Arizona Republic

101

Spitzer Scandal

The Eliot Spitzer scandal came out of left field, to the horror of Americans (and the delight of cartoonists). Federal agents caught New York Governor Spitzer over a wiretap arranging to meet a prostitute named Ashley Dupré; he had spent up to $80,000 on "high-class" prostitutes. Spitzer resigned as governor, with his wife loyally standing by his side, followed by a torrent of headlines and extremely unflattering cartoons.   Dupré tried to leverage the attention to further her singing career. It is a cartoonist's dream that every politician has a secret as dark as Eliot Spitzer and a MySpace page as entertaining as Ashley Dupré's.

DARYL CAGLE
MSNBC.COM

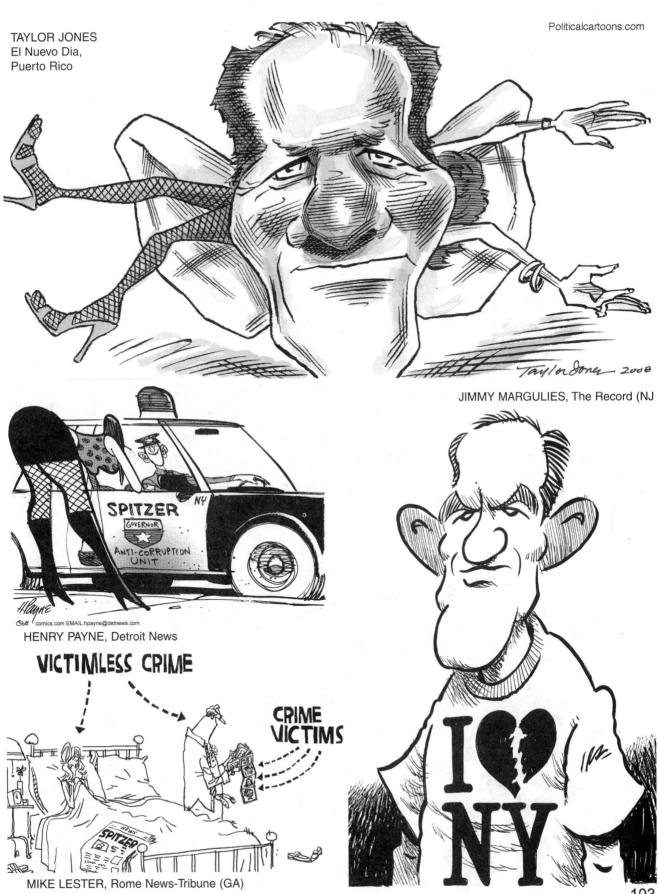

TAYLOR JONES
El Nuevo Dia,
Puerto Rico

HENRY PAYNE, Detroit News

JIMMY MARGULIES, The Record (NJ

VICTIMLESS CRIME

CRIME VICTIMS

MIKE LESTER, Rome News-Tribune (GA)

103

SHERFFIUS Boulder Camera © 3/11/08 COPLEY NEWS SERVICE jsherffius@aol.com

JOHN SHERFFIUS
Boulder Daily Camera

NATE BEELER
Washington Examiner

BILL DAY, Memphis Commercial Appeal

DANA SUMMERS, Orlando Sentinel

DON WRIGHT, Palm Beach Post

105

MIKE LUCKOVICH, The Atlanta Journal-Constitution

MikeLuckovich
ATLANTA JOURNAL-CONSTITUTION ©
AJC.com 3-14-8

ELIOT SPITZER MAKES GOOD ON HIS PROMISE TO CLEAN UP NEW YORK'S GOVERNMENT.

GOV. OFFICE

JOHN COLE, Scranton Times-Tribune

MICHAEL RAMIREZ, Investors Business Daily

DAN WASSERMAN
Boston Globe

MIKE LESTER
Rome News-Tribune, GA

DARIO CASTILLEJOS, Mexico

107

HIS OWN PETARD

STEVE SACK
Minneapolis
Star-Tribune

ROBERT ARIAIL
The State, SC

GARY BROOKINS, Richmond Times-Dispatch

JOHN DEERING, Arkansas Democrat Gazette

PASSING THE TORCH...

ADAM ZYGLIS, Buffalo News

PAT BAGLEY, Salt Lake Tribune, UT

BOB GORRELL

"HOW ABOUT A LITTLE ROLE PLAYING? YOU BE THE HIGH-PRICED CALL GIRL AND I'LL BE THE SANCTIMONIOUS GASBAG."

DREW SHENEMAN, Newark Star Ledger

DAVID HORSEY, Seattle Post Intelligencer

WALT HANDELSMAN
Newsday

MATT BORS, Idiot Box

SEX SCANDAL CHEAT SHEET

POLITICIANS: CLIP OUT COMIC. KEEP IN YOUR POCKET. REFER TO OFTEN.

HOW MUCH TROUBLE ARE YOU IN?

YOU'RE HAVING AN "IMPROPER RELATIONSHIP" WITH A...	WILL YOU GO TO JAIL?	IS YOUR CAREER OVER?
CUTE INTERN	NO	LOL
CALL GIRL	IF YOU HAVE ENEMIES IN HIGH PLACES	MAYBE
DUDE IN A BATHROOM	DEPENDS HOW FAR ALONG YOU WERE WHEN CAUGHT	SURPRISINGLY, NO
TEENAGE BOY	DEFINITELY	ME THINKS SO
SEA CUCUMBER	DEPENDS ON THE STATE	AGAIN, DEPENDS ON THE STATE

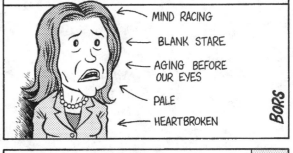

THINK ABOUT THE WIFE (REMEMBER HER?). WHEN MAKING A PUBLIC APOLOGY, DON'T FORCE YOUR SHELL-SHOCKED WOMAN TO STAND BESIDE YOU.

← MIND RACING
← BLANK STARE
← AGING BEFORE OUR EYES
← PALE
← HEARTBROKEN

BORS

CONSIDERING A DENIAL? DON'T USE THESE:

I'M NOT GAY.

I WOULD **NEVER** PAY THAT MUCH FOR SEX!

I DID NOT HAVE SEXUAL RELATIONS WITH THAT SEA CUCUMBER!

Russia vs. Georgia

The quick, brutal military conflict between Georgia and Russia took the world by surprise. Georgia claimed Russia was trying to reunite the old Soviet Union, while Russia countered that Georgia was oppressing enclaves of Russians living in Georgia, and the Bush administration may have encouraged Georgia to provoke their nasty neighbor. Of course, Russia being the traditional bad guys, were the easiest to blame–and caricature. While McCain claimed, "We are all Georgians," on the campaign trail, cartoonists drew bloodthirsty bears and Vladimir Putin's hungry eyes.

SHERFFIUS
Boulder Camera © 8/11/08
CREATORS SYNDICATE
jsherffius@aol.com

JOHN SHERFFIUS
Boulder Daily Camera

GEORGIA
Tskhinvali
Gori
Tbilisi

BRIAN ADCOCK
Scotland

113

GARY MARKSTEIN

I KNEW YOU'D NEVER LEAVE ME.

GEORGIA, WE WILL BURY YOU

PUTIN

IT WAS SELF DEFENSE!

RUSSIA

BOB GORRELL

BRUTALITY

STEVE SACK
Minneapolis
Star-Tribune

GEORGIA

RUSSIA VS. GEORGIA

MICHAEL RAMIREZ
Investors Business Daily

IT WAS "SELF DEFENSE."

WWW.IBDeditorials.com/cartoons

manfrancisco@yahoo.com
The Manila Times
AUG1009
SKP

REPUBLIC OF GEORGIA

MANNY FRANCISCO
Manila, Phillipines

STEVE GREENBERG, Ventura County Star

SCOTT STANTIS, Birmingham News

CHIP BOK, Akron Beacon-Journal

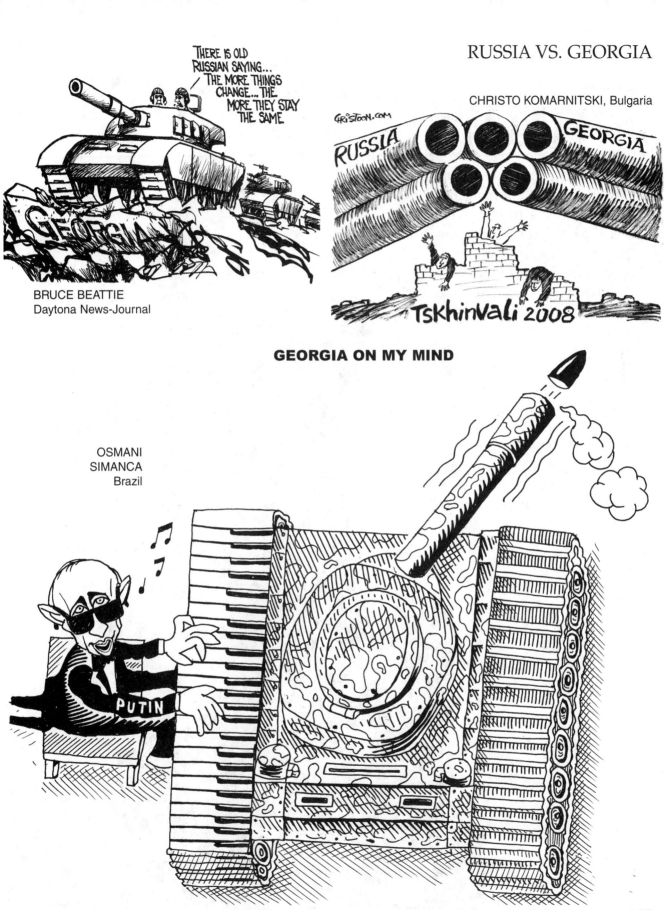

BRUCE BEATTIE
Daytona News-Journal

CHRISTO KOMARNITSKI, Bulgaria

OSMANI
SIMANCA
Brazil

GEORGIA ON MY MIND

Chinese Olympics

The summer games are usually a U.S. show, start to finish, and Michael Phelps' historic 8-gold medal performance this year made the Beijing competition no exception. But this year, while America did come away from the Beijing summer games with its usual #1 spot in total medals, China got the most golds and came in a close second overall.

The Olympics were not free from their fair share of controversy, though. Between underage Chinese gymnasts and Phelps' monster torso, there was no shortage of sporty cartoon fodder.

ANGEL BOLIGAN
El Universal
Mexico

RIBER HANSSON
Sweden

NATE BEELER, Washington Examiner

MARSHALL RAMSEY
Clarion Ledger (MI)

119

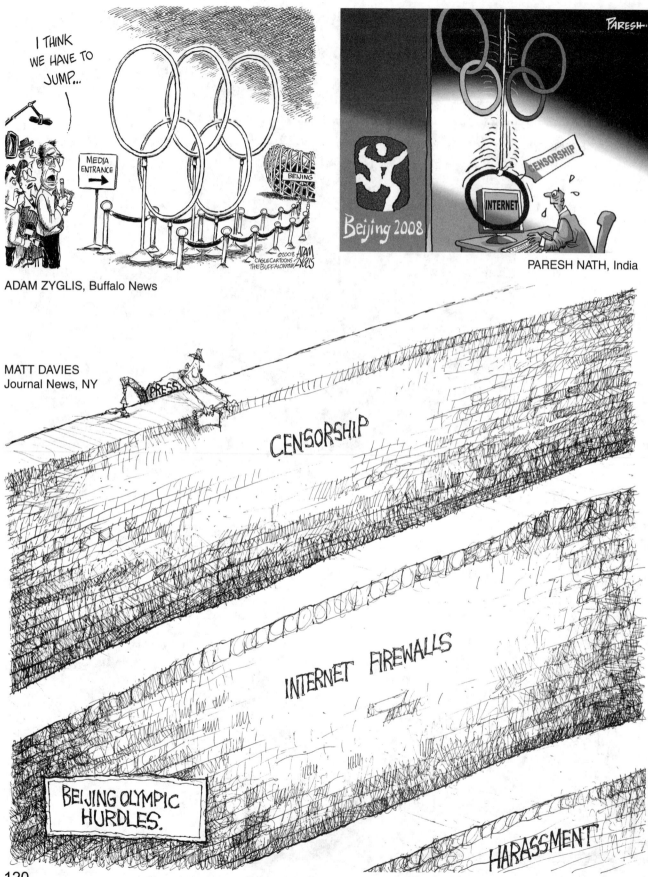

ADAM ZYGLIS, Buffalo News

PARESH NATH, India

MATT DAVIES
Journal News, NY

120

BEIJING POLLUTION

STEVE BREEN
San Diego Union Tribune

ROBERT ARIAIL, The State, SC

DWANE POWELL, Raliegh News & Observer

STEVE SACK, Minneapolis Star-Tribune

OLYMPIC WELCOMING COMMITTEE

INGRID RICE, British Columbia, Canada

FREDERICK DELIGNE, Nice-Matin, France

RICHARD CROWSON, Witchita Eagle

BILL DAY, Memphis Commercial Appeal

PATRICK O'CONNOR, Los Angeles Daily News

MIKE KEEFE, Denver Post

www.caglecartoons.com

BRIAN DUFFY, The Des Moines Register

GARY BROOKINS, The Richmond Times-Dispatch

CHINA'S GOLD IN WOMEN'S GYMNASTICS

DANA SUMMERS, Orlando Sentinel

STEVE BREEN, San Diego Union Tribune

STEPHANE PERAY, Thailand

CHIP BOK, Akron Beacon-Journal

RANDY BISH, Pittsburgh Tribune-Review

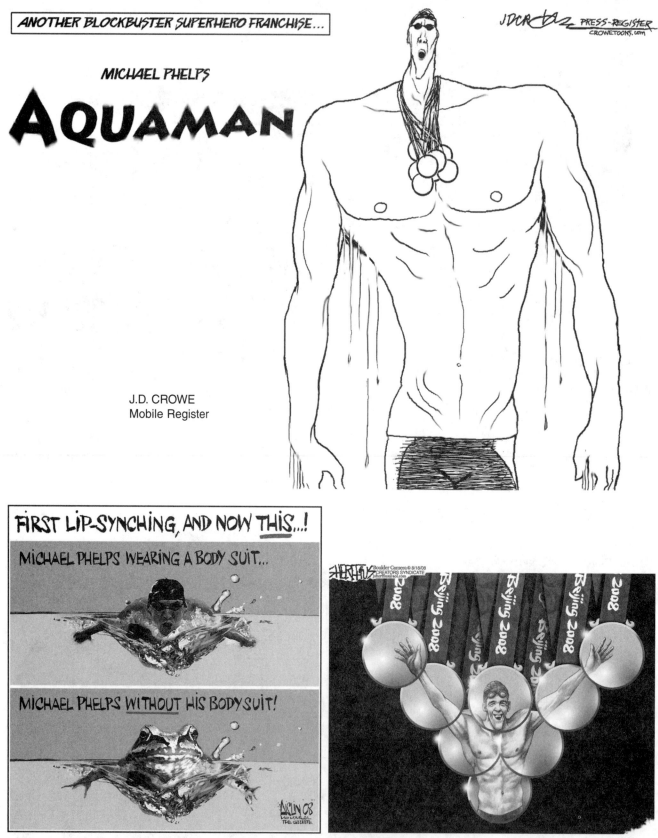

ANOTHER BLOCKBUSTER SUPERHERO FRANCHISE...

MICHAEL PHELPS

AQUAMAN

J.D. CROWE
Mobile Register

PRESS-REGISTER
CROWETOONS.com

FIRST LIP-SYNCHING, AND NOW THIS...!

MICHAEL PHELPS WEARING A BODY SUIT...

MICHAEL PHELPS WITHOUT HIS BODYSUIT!

TERRY "AISLIN" MOSHER, Montreal Gazette

JOHN SHERFFIUS, Boulder Daily Camera

DARYL CAGLE
MSNBC.COM

JACK OHMAN
Portland Oregonian

127

THE AMAZING MICHAEL PHELPS HEADS BACK FROM BEIJING TO AMERICA.

DAVID FITZSIMMONS, Arizona Daily Star

OH GOD... ALL THOSE GOLD MEDALS... HE OVERBALANCED AND SANK TO THE BOTTOM!

VINCE O'FARRELL, Illawarra Mercury, Australia

ENDORSEMENTS

STEVE KELLEY, New Orleans Times-Picayune

EVOLUTION OF MICHAEL PHELPS...

JEFF STAHLER, Columbus Dispatch

MICHAEL PHELPS...

STEVE BREEN, San Diego Union Tribune

MICHAEL PHELPS

OK, THIS IS GETTING HUMILIATING....

MIKE LUCKOVICH, The Atlanta Journal-Constitution

FREDERICK DELIGNE, Nice-Matin, France

Gay Marriage

In an historic and controversial decision, the California Supreme Court upheld the rights of gays to marry in the state. Conservatives freaked out. Were we seeing activist judges, or actual justice? Cartoonists were politically split, but even many of those on the side of "non-traditional marriage" took the easy way out with gags.

ADAM ZYGLIS
Buffalo News

NATE BEELER
Washington Examiner

JEFF STAHLER
Columbus Dispatch

MIKE THOMPSON, Detroit Free-Press

ATTACK OF THE HACKS!

MATT BORS, Idiot Box

132

DARYL CAGLE, MSNBC.COM

JOHN SHERFFIUS
Boulder Daily Camera

A state of enlightenment

JOHN SHERFFIUS, Boulder Daily Camera

ANYONE BESIDES THE PEOPLE OF CALIFORNIA, THAT IS!

CHUCK ASAY
Colorado Springs Gazette

CALIFORNIA SUPREME COURT

I NOW PRONOUNCE YOU, "HUSBAND AND WHATEVER!"

© 2008 CREATORS SYNDICATE, INC.

JOE HELLER
Green Bay Press Gazette

MARK STREETER, Savannah Morning News

HOW GAY MARRIAGE THREATENS HETEROSEXUAL MARRIAGE

WE CAN'T COMPETE WITH THIS !!!

MIKE LUCKOVICH
The Atlanta
Journal-Constitution

GAY MARRIAGE

STEVE BENSON
Arizona Republic

MIKE LESTER
Rome News-
Tribune (GA)

IN OTHER NEWS, CALIFORNIA LEGALIZED GAY MARRIAGE TODAY...

BRIAN FAIRRINGTON
Cagle Cartoons

I'm leaving you for someone else...

CALIFORNIA

Traditional Family Values

JIMMY MARGULIES, The Record (NJ)

Hey, we didn't hire a videographer for the wedding...

It's a Republican attack ad...

Same Sex Marriage

CAMPAIGN 2008

Housing Crisis

DARYL CAGLE
MSNBC.COM

After years of dangerously inflated house prices, the real estate market tumbled and then took a nosedive. Thousands of Americans with subprime mortgages and homes that they couldn't afford faced foreclosure at the hands of greedy lenders. The rental market was crushed with a sudden influx of tenants; prices rose. Suddenly, even debt-free employed newlyweds couldn't get a decent mortgage. And the government's huge bailouts for Fannie Mae and Freddie Mac only helped the guys who had perpetrated the subprime debacle in the first place. For some cartoonists, it all hit close to home.

PATRICK O'CONNOR, Los Angeles Daily News

JIMMY MARGULIES, The Record (NJ

JEFF PARKER, Florida Today

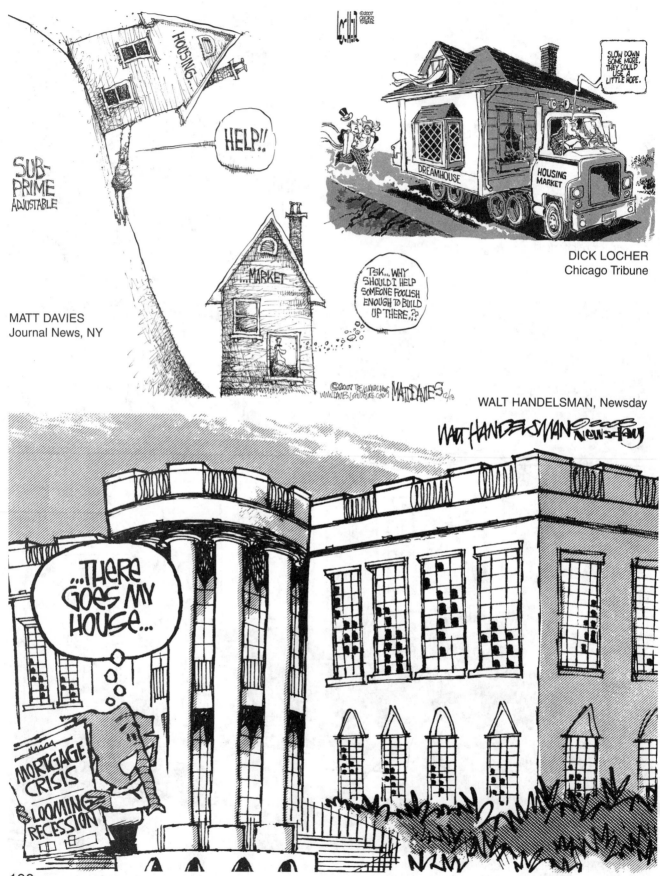

MATT DAVIES
Journal News, NY

DICK LOCHER
Chicago Tribune

WALT HANDELSMAN, Newsday

ARES
Cuba

ARES.

GARY MARKSTEIN

BILL DAY, Memphis Commercial Appeal

MIKE LANE
Cagle Cartoons

STEVE KELLEY, New Orleans Times-Picayune

MIKE LANE, Cagle Cartoons

NATE BEELER, Washington Examiner

GARY VARVEL, Indianapolis Star

MILT PRIGGEE, Politicalcartoons.com

ARCADIO ESQUIVEL
La Prensa, Panama

143

Fannie Mae and Freddie Mac

They were the first to fall in the long trail of financial market dominos this year. When the federal government stepped in and took over failing loan giants Fanny Mae and Freddie Mac, the markets took a deep breath and plunged. The millions in severance Fannie and Freddie paid to their CEOs? Just icing on the cake. But as citizens and cartoonists alike were soon to find out, it was only the first of a series of financial blunders to pummel the economy.

MICHAEL RAMIREZ, Investors Business Daily

THE OTHER SHOES TO DROP...

R.J. MATSON
St. Louis Post Dispatch

JOE HELLER, Green Bay Press Gazette

"National health insurance? Now that would be wrong."
CAL GRONDAHL, Utah Standard Examiner

145

FANNIE MAE AND FREDDIE MAC

GARY VARVEL
Indianapolis Star

DAN WASSERMAN, Boston Globe

DANA SUMMERS, Orlando Sentinel

ROBERT ARIAIL
The State, SC

ETTA ©2008 ETTATORIALS
HULME

FREDDIE MAC AND FANNIE MAE
MOVE BACK IN WITH THE FOLKS

ETTA HULME
Ft. Worth
Star-Telegram

FANNIE and FREDDIE MOVE IN...

YOU GONNA FINISH ALL THAT?

TAX PAYER

MIKE LANE, Cagle Cartoons

BRUCE BEATTIE
Daytona News-Journal

"So, let me get this straight . . . I'm paying off my mortgages to Fannie and
Freddie, and bailing 'em out with my tax money at the same time?!"

FANNIE MAE AND FREDDIE MAC

CHIP BOK
Akron
Beacon-
Journal

PARESH NATH, India

DAVID FITZSIMMONS, Arizona Daily Star

NATE BEELER
Washington Examiner

STEVE BENSON
Arizona Republic

Wall Street CRASH!

It took Washington by surprise, but some economists had been predicting the economic collapse for nearly a year. Still, when banks began folding and the credit market seized up, the Wall Street house of cards fell down on Main Street. The Dow lurched below 9,000 points, to where it was ten years earlier. It seemed to be the end of an era of greed at the same time that tax dollars were being redirected for fat cats' golden parachutes and expensive vacations.

PATRICK CHAPPATTE, International Herald Tribune

STEVE BREEN
San Diego Union Tribune

FREDERICK DELIGNE, Nice-Matin, France

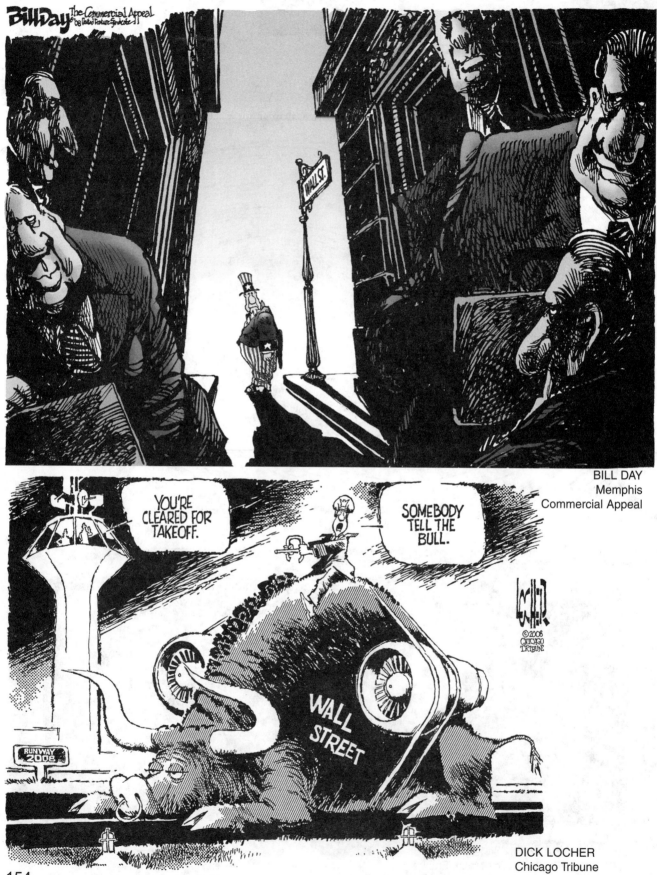

BILL DAY
Memphis
Commercial Appeal

DICK LOCHER
Chicago Tribune

WALL STREET CRASH!

...RELAX, MY BROKER SAYS THE ECONOMY WILL BOUNCE BACK...

...I AM YOUR BROKER!...

WALL ST

WORK FOR FOOD

WALT HANDELSMAN
Newsday

DARYL CAGLE, MSNBC.COM

BANK

BARACK OBAMA PALS AROUND WITH A TERRORIST, YOU KNOW.

JIHO
France

155

MICHAEL RAMIREZ, Investors Business Daily

MIKE KEEFE, Denver Post

NATE BEELER, Washington Examiner

DON WRIGHT, Palm Beach Post

SANDY HUFFAKER
Cagle Cartoons

WALL STREET CRASH!

RANDY BISH
Pittsburgh Tribune-Review

VINCE O'FARRELL
Illawarra Mercury, Australia

ANGEL BOLIGAN
El Universal Mexico

PARESH NATH, India

157

BRIAN ADCOCK, Scotland

MARSHALL RAMSEY, Clarion Ledger (MI)

ARES
Cuba

158

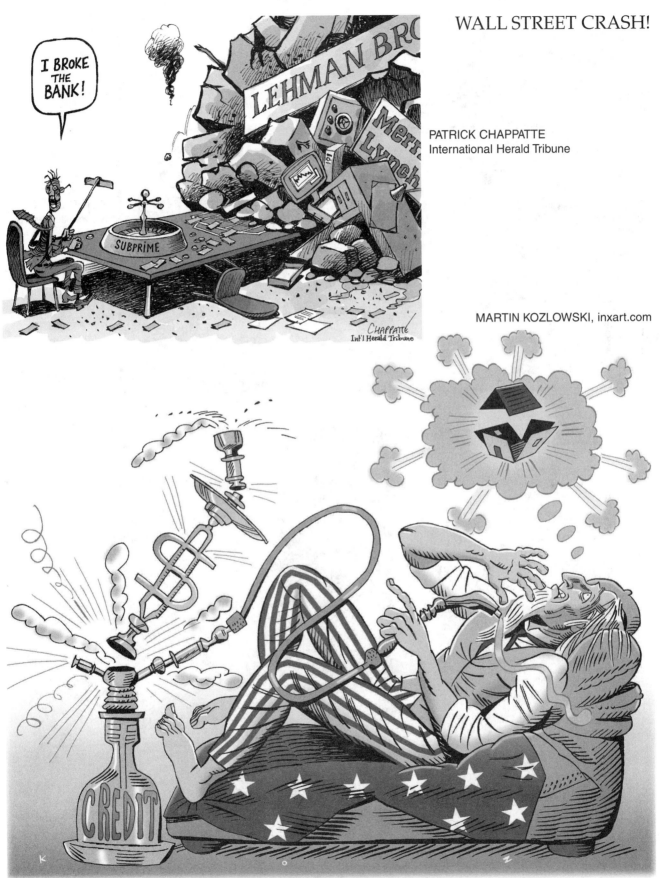

WALL STREET CRASH!

PATRICK CHAPPATTE
International Herald Tribune

MARTIN KOZLOWSKI, inxart.com

PETER LEWIS
Newcastle Herald
Australia

JOHN COLE
Scranton
Times-Tribune

'IS IT TOO LATE TO PUT HIM BACK TOGETHER AGAIN?'

HUMPTY DUMPTY SAT ON A WALL...

MORTGAGE SECURITIES

WALL STREET

CRUNCH

HUMPTY DUMPTY HAD A... HAD.. A...

OH, NEVERMIND.

WALL STREET CRASH!

R.J. MATSON, St. Louis Post Dispatch

PAT BAGLEY, Salt Lake Tribune (UT)

DARYL CAGLE
MSNBC.com

JOHN DARKOW
Columbia Daily
Tribune (MO)

PETER NICHOLSON, The Australian, Sydney

JOHN TREVER, Albuquerque Journal

VINCE O'FARRELL, Illawarra Mercury, Australia

JACK OHMAN, Portland Oregonian

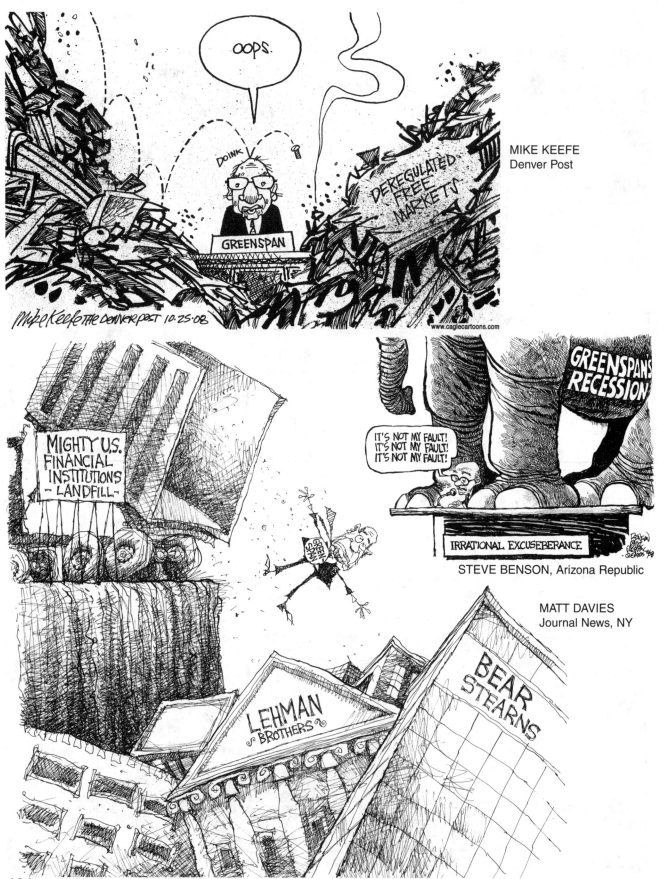

MIKE KEEFE
Denver Post

STEVE BENSON, Arizona Republic

MATT DAVIES
Journal News, NY

ADAM ZYGLIS, Buffalo News

PARESH NATH, India

R.J. MATSON, St. Louis Post Dispatch

BRUCE BEATTIE, Daytona News-Journal

ROB ROGERS, Pittsburgh Post-Gazette

Wall Street BAILOUT!

When the credit markets froze, Washington started moving some big money. The "Wall Street Bailout" rocketed through congress, authorizing over $700 billion to be spent loosening the credit markets back up. President Bush insisted that a failure to pass the bailout would be a disaster. To pass the bill in a hurry, congress gilded it with pork. Of course, the credit markets ground to a halt because greedy Wall Street lenders gave too much credit to people who were not creditworthy—but what the heck, more credit must be a good thing. The massive cost of the bailout was equivalent to the cost of the war in Iraq, or twice as much as it would cost to give universal health care to every American. Most Americans resented the idea of bailing out mega-rich Wall Street fat cats.

DARYL CAGLE
MSNBC.com

167

JOHN COLE
Scranton Times-Tribune

JACK OHMAN, Portland Oregonian

JIM DAY, Las Vegas Review Journal

ERIC DEVERICKS, Seattle Times

MIKE KEEFE, Denver Post

WALL STREET BAILOUT!

GOP 2008 CONGRESSIONAL RACES

©MATSON
caglecartoons.com ROLL CALL

R.J. MATSON
St. Louis Post Dispatch

NIK SCOTT, Australia

well, he looks shifty to me ...

171

RANDY BISH, Pittsburgh Tribune-Review

MARK STREETER, Savannah Morning News

WAYNE STAYSKAL

WALL STREET BAILOUT!

MIKE LANE
Cagle Cartoons

www.CAGLECARTOONS.com

MARTIN KOZLOWSKI
inxart.com

Bank Bailout Backlash

DWAYNE BOOTH, Mr. Fish

173

VINCE O'FARRELL, Illawarra Mercury, Australia

ANDY SINGER
No Exit

JOHN TREVER, Albuquerque Journal

WALL STREET BAILOUT!

JOHN TREVER
Albuquerque Journal

J.D. CROWE
Mobile Register

Senator Stevens

Senator Ted Stevens was convicted of lying about gifts and remodeling on his house, scooping up swag from people who had an … erm … interest in what the senator could do for them. The powerful Alaska legislator was the longest serving Republican senator and was most famous for "earmark" pork barrel spending, including the infamous "Bridge to Nowhere." Stevens ran for re-election while he was on trial and was likely to win a tight race, only to face possible explusion from the Senate.

The Bridge to Nowhere

RANDY BISH, Pittsburgh Tribune-Review

THE FINAL GIFT

TO: SEN. TED STEVENS
FROM: THE JURY

GUILTY VERDICT

KIRK WALTERS, Toledo Blade

R.J. MATSON, St. Louis Post Dispatch

BIG **A** mart
ALASKA
POLITICIANS CONSIGNMENT STORE

SARAH PALIN'S CAMPAIGN COUTURE
$10⁰⁰
DESIGNER SHOES

SEN. TED STEVENS HOME FURNISHINGS CLOSE OUT
MASSAGE CHAIR LOANER
VIKING GRILL

BRIDGE TO NOWHERE
SALE

SARAH PALIN TRAVEL PACKAGE
*KIDS, HUSBANDS, RELATIVES
FLY FREE!

caglecartoons.com © MATSON
ST. LOUIS POST-DISPATCH

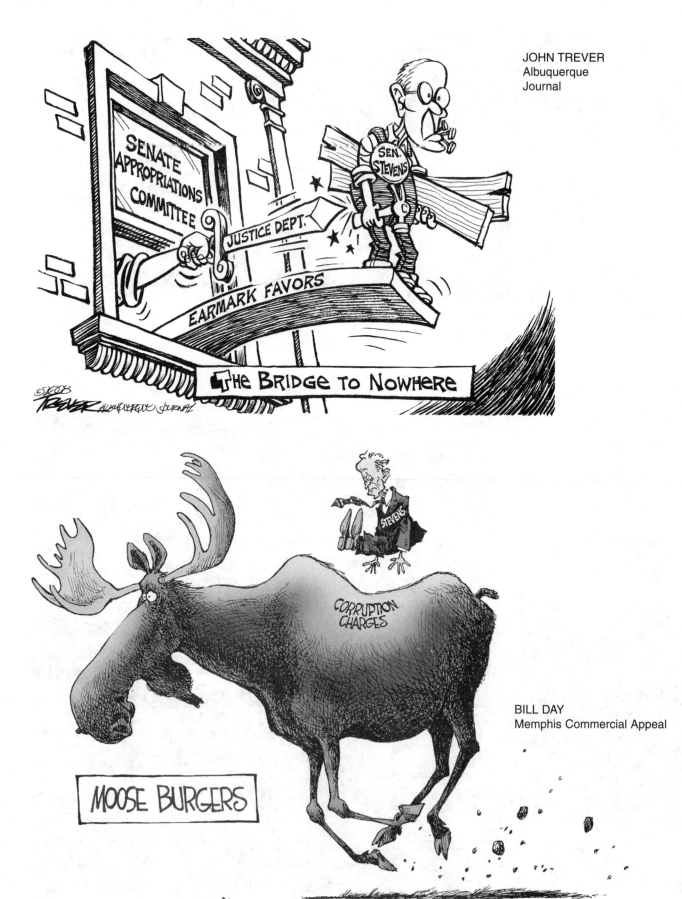

JOHN TREVER
Albuquerque
Journal

SENATE APPROPRIATIONS COMMITTEE

JUSTICE DEPT.

EARMARK FAVORS

THE BRIDGE TO NOWHERE

SEN. STEVENS

STEVENS

CORRUPTION CHARGES

MOOSE BURGERS

BILL DAY
Memphis Commercial Appeal

JIMMY MARGULIES, The Record (NJ)

CHIP BOK
Akron Beacon-Journal

PATRICK O'CONNOR
Los Angeles Daily News

179

Bush's Legacy

It was a lame duck year for President George W. Bush. But while George W. Bush might not have gotten a lot done in the way of legislation, he sure made history—many thought he was our worst president ever. His approval ratings hovered around 30 percent. But his eight years of stubborn, short-sighted policies will have lasting effects for the American people and the next administration for an even longer time to come. Plus cartoonists who'd perfected Bush's beady eyes and fleshy ears had to fit in their last cowboy caricatures before W. left office.

THOMAS BOLDT
Calgary Sun

NATE BEELER
Washington Examiner

DARYL CAGLE
MSNBC.COM

BILL DAY, Memphis Commercial Appeal

BUSH'S LEGACY

JUSTIN BILICKI

BRUCE BEATTIE, Daytona News-Journal

STAR TRIBUNE
sack

STEVE SACK
Minneapolis
Star-Tribune

THEN AGAIN, MAYBE THE PROBLEM ISN'T THE <u>TRACK</u>...

U.S. ON WRONG TRACK — POLL

BUSH WAR

BUSH ECONOMY

MIKE LUCKOVICH, The Atlanta Journal-Constitution

YOU QUIT GOLF AND PUT YOUR CLUBS IN STORAGE TO HONOR U.S. TROOPS KILLED IN IRAQ? YOU MUST THINK OF THEM OFTEN....

YEP. ESPECIALLY MY PUTTER....

IF YOU WON'T PLAY 'LEGACY', I'M TAKING MY BALL HOME!

I'LL PLAY

MICHAEL McPARLANE, Politicalcartoons.com

184

ROB ROGERS, Pittsburgh Post-Gazette

MIKE LANE, Cagle Cartoons

ROB ROGERS, Pittsburgh Post-Gazette

"NOT TO WORRY — I'M OKAY!"

PAT BAGLEY
Salt Lake Tribune (UT)

TAYLOR JONES
El Nuevo Dia
Puerto Rico

187

The Candidates

The presidential race started off with a wide field of candidates on both sides. The early frontrunners were Democratic Senator Hillary Clinton and Republican Mayor Rudy Giuliani, who fizzled fast. Hillary fought a long and bitter battle against a better funded and better organized Barack Obama, losing the race just before the Democratic Convention.

The also-ran candidates didn't amount to much, and most of them didn't even raise their profiles enough to be featured in cartoons by themselves. There was some excitement when sleepy Senator Fred Thompson entered the race, only to drift away. Mitt Romney held on for a while, but his flip-flop on the abortion issue, and his Mormon religion were tough sells to the GOP's evangelical base. Except for Hillary, the losing candidates didn't amount to much.

DARYL CAGLE, MSNBC.com

SANDY HUFFAKER, Cagle Cartoons

BOB GORRELL

MIKE LUCKOVICH, Atlanta Journal-Constitution

189

THE CANDIDATES

MIKE RAMIREZ, Investors Business Daily

ERIC DEVERICKS
Seattle Times

DAVID HORSEY
Seattle Post Intelligencer

DWANE POWELL
Raliegh News & Observer

CHIP BOK
Akron Beacon-Journal

191

GRAEME MACKAY

DAN WASSERMAN, Boston Globe

DWANE POWELL, Raliegh News & Observer

HILLARY'S SECURITY DETAIL

GARY BROOKINS
The Richmond Times-Dispatch

MIKE RAMIREZ
Investors Business Daily

ROBERT ARIAIL
The State, SC

STEVE BENSON, Arizona Republic

ROBERT ARIAIL, The State (SC)

DAN WASSERMAN
Boston Globe

MARSHALL RAMSEY
Clarion Ledger (MI)

ED STEIN
Rocky Mountain News

GARY BROOKINS, The Richmond Times-Dispatch

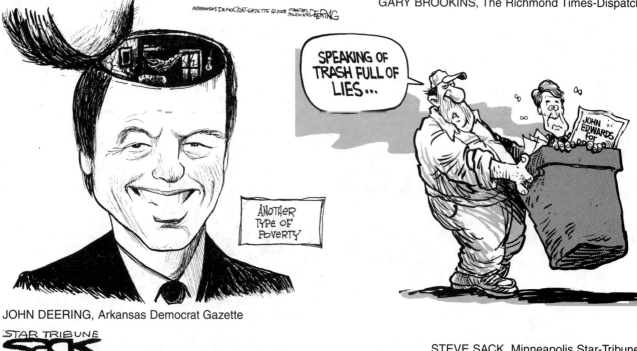

JOHN DEERING, Arkansas Democrat Gazette

STEVE SACK, Minneapolis Star-Tribune

REX BABIN, Sacramento Bee

JOHN EDWARDS BOWS OUT
SCOTT STANTIS, Birmingham News

CHUCK ASAY, Colorado Springs Gazette

ROB ROGERS
Pittsburgh Post-Gazette

SCOTT STANTIS
Birmingham News

199

Barack Obama

Barack Obama splashed onto the scene after only two years in the Senate. He filled stadiums across the country with adoring supporters that dwarfed the crowds that John McCain could draw. Republicans derided Obama as a "celebrity" and called him the "messiah."

Obama hit some bumps along the way; his beloved preacher, Jeremiah Wright, dominated YouTube.com and Fox News with offensive sermons that led Obama to leave the church. The GOP tried tying Obama to a voter registration scandal involving a group called ACORN, without much success.

Eventually, even Republican, Secretary of State, General Colin Powell endorsed Obama.

Obama seemed unstoppable.

TAYLOR JONES
Politicalcartoons.com

ANGEL BOLIGAN
El Universal
Mexico

STEVE NEASE, Oakville Beaver (Canada)

JERRY HOLBERT, Boston Herald

ROBERT ARIAIL
The State (SC)

DANA SUMMERS, Orlando Sentinel

JEFF KOTERBA, Omaha World Herald

FIRST PRESIDENTIAL DEBATE...

JEFF STAHLER
Columbus Dispatch

THE AUDACITY OF A DOPE

STEVE SACK
Minneapolis Star-Tribune

STEVE GREENBERG
Ventura County Star

RAINER HACHFELD, Germany

STEVE BENSON
Arizona Republic

STEVE KELLEY
New Orleans Times-Picayune

MIKE LUCKOVICH
Atlanta Journal-Constitution

BRIAN DUFFY
Des Moines Register

JERRY HOLBERT, Boston Herald

BILL DAY, Memphis Commercial Appeal

THE RUNNING MATE

MARSHALL RAMSEY, Clarion Ledger, MI

OBAMAFLAK...

IS HE WEARING A FLAG LAPEL PIN?

HIS PASTOR IS A RACIST...

WASN'T HIS MOTHER A COMMUNIST?

WHAT DOES HE MEAN... "REFINING" HIS IRAQ POLICY?

HE HAS NO EXPERIENCE BEING PRESIDENT.

IS HE SINGING THE NATIONAL ANTHEM?

IS HIS HAND ON HIS CHEST?

HE'S SUPPORTING GRANTS TO FAITH-BASED GROUPS?

I DON'T THINK HE CAN LEGALLY BE PRESIDENT, CAN HE?

IS HE FLIP-FLOPPING ON ABORTION?

ISN'T HE A MUSLIM?

..SIGH..

THANK TO KANDY CATE

caglecartoons.com

© 2008 MONTE WOLVERTON

MONTE WOLVERTON, Cagle Cartoons

205

JIANPING FAN, China

CHUCK ASAY, Colorado Springs Gazette

JOHN DEERING, Arkansas Democrat Gazette

INGRID RICE, British Columbia, Canada

THE POLITICS OF CHAINS

SCOTT STANTIS
Birmingham News

ERIC ALLIE, Politicalcartoons.com

JUSTIN BILICKI

IN THE SPOTLIGHT

207

NATE BEELER, Washington Examiner

STEVE SACK
Minneapolis Star-Tribune

THE NUT DOESN'T FALL FAR FROM THE TREE
RANDY BISH, Pittsburgh Tribune-Review

JEFF STAHLER
Columbus Dispatch

STEVE BENSON, Arizona Republic

RANDY BISH
Pittsburgh Tribune-Review

GARY MCCOY
Cagle Cartoons

STEVE GREENBERG, Ventura County Star

CHRISTO KOMARNITSKI, Bulgaria

TAYLOR JONES
Politicalcartoons.com

209

John McCain

John McCain had a wild ride to the Republican nomination. His campaign seemed to have run out of gas when he came back strong to win the primaries. Then, falling behind Obama in the polls, he made the bold choice of Sarah Palin, who gave him a brief bump in the polls before becoming a late night, talk show joke.

Cartoonists pounced on McCain for being old, and took joy in drawing his crazy neck. McCain seemed hot and angry compared to cool Obama, often flip-flopping to whatever position seemed to give a boost in that day's polls. He abruptly stopped his campaign to focus on the economic crisis. He moved from one theme to another, accusing Obama of associating with terrorists, saying Obama would raise taxes on "Joe the Plumber;" McCain never quite found his footing in the general election.

TAYLOR JONES
Politicalcartoons.com

DID I TELL YOU PERTY GALS I WAS A MAVERICK?

TAYLOR JONES
El Nuevo Dia, Puerto Rico

JACK OHMAN
Portland Oregonian

GEORGE W. McCAIN

DAVID HORSEY, Seattle Post Intelligencer

211

"STILL, SEN. McCAIN CAN SOMETIMES BETRAY HIS LEGENDARY TEMPER."

HENRY PAYNE, Detroit News

SCOTT STANTIS, Birmingham News

JoineD AT the HiP

STEVE SACK, Minneapolis Star-Tribune

LARRY WRIGHT, Detroit News

JOHN DARKOW
Columbia Daily
Tribune, MO

JOHN SHERFFIUS, Boulder Daily Camera

PATRICK O'CONNOR
Los Angeles Daily News

MATT DAVIES
Journal News, NY

JOHN COLE, Scranton Times-Tribune

is   a   wealthy   elitist.

McCain #5   McCain #6   McCain #7   McCain #8

GARY BROOKINS
The Richmond Times-Dispatch

GARY MARKSTEIN

ANDY SINGER, No Exit

MARSHALL RAMSEY, Clarion Ledger (MI)

HENRY PAYNE
Detroit News

BILL SCHORR

"CAN YOU MAKE HIM LOOK YOUNGER AND HER LOOK OLDER ?..."

215

JOHN COLE
Scranton Times-Tribune

BRIAN FAIRRINGTON
Cagle Cartoons

WAYNE STAYSKAL

DAVID FITZSIMMONS
Arizona Daily Star

JOHN DARKOW
Columbia Daily
Tribune (MO)

JOHN COLE, Scranton Times-Tribune

NATE BEELER, Washington Examiner

MIKE KEEFE, Denver Post

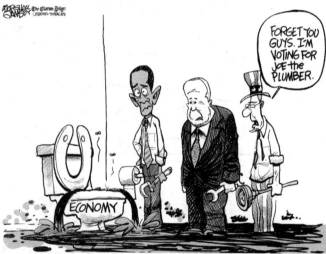

MARSHALL RAMSEY, Clarion Ledger (MI)

SCOTT STANTIS, Birmingham News

ADAM ZYGLIS, Buffalo News

218

HOW THOSE STINKY POLITICAL CAMPAIGN ROBOCALLS WORK

"HI-THIS IS JOE THE PLUMBER..."

JIM DAY
Las Vegas
Review Journal

Jim Day '08 LAS VEGAS REVIEW-JOURNAL

TAYLOR JONES
El Nuevo Dia
Puerto Rico

YEAH, LOOKS LIKE WE'RE GOING TO NEED THAT PLUMBER AGAIN. NAH—SAME OLD PROBLEM.

Taylor Jones 2008

Palin's Bid for V.P.

With his campaign sagging, John McCain made the bold choice of Alaska Governor Sarah Palin as his running mate. Palin, a pretty, new face on the GOP scene, soon stole the show and was the focus of media attention for two months, exciting conservatives and late night comics. First, we learned about Palin's unwed, pregnant teenage daughter, Bristol. Then Palin seemed to lack knowledge of world issues as we learned that she only recently applied for her first passport, had never met a foreign leader, and was seen in strange YouTube videos in her Pentacostal church. She muffed TV interviews and was ridiculed on Saturday Night Live as she cited her foreign policy experience as "you can see Russia from Alaska." Palin was a hit at the convention, with a joke:

    Q: *"What is the difference between a pitbull and a hockey mom?"*
    A: *"Lipstick."*

When Obama made a reference to "lipstick on a pig" the Republicans feigned outrage that Obama would call Palin a "pig." We learned that the GOP spent $150,000 on clothes for Palin and her children. Palin was dogged by a scandal in Alaska,"Troopergate," where she fired an official who wouldn't fire her ex-brother-in-law, who was involved in a messy divorce with her sister. After the election, a McCain staffer described the Palins as "Alaska hillbillies." With Palin's crazy family and one gaffe after another, she was a treasure for cartoonists.

Dwayne Booth, Mr. Fish

PATRICK CORRIGAN, Toronto Star

TAYLOR JONES, Politicalcartoons.com

DARYL CAGLE
MSNBC.COM

221

STEVE BREEN, San Diego Union Tribune

MIKE RAMIREZ
Investors Business Daily

JOHN COLE
Scranton Times-Tribune

222

PALIN'S BID FOR V.P.

PATRICK O'CONNOR, Los Angeles Daily News

CHIP BOK
Akron Beacon-Journal

BOKBLUSTER.COM ©08 AKRON BEACON JOURNAL

CAMERON CARDOW, Ottawa Citizen (Canada)

KIRK WALTERS, Toledo Blade

BILL DAY, Memphis Commercial Appeal

RANIER HACHFELD, Germany

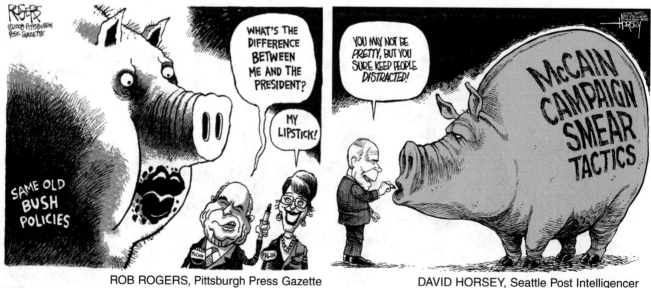

ROB ROGERS, Pittsburgh Press Gazette

DAVID HORSEY, Seattle Post Intelligencer

DREW SHENEMAN
Newark Star Ledger

DON WRIGHT
Palm Beach Post

STEVE NEASE, Oakville Beaver (Canada)

DARYL CAGLE
MSNBC.COM

JOHN SHERFFIUS
Boulder Daily Camera

BRIDGE TO NOWHERE...

LIES DISTORTIONS INEXPERIENCE

PALIN

ROB ROGERS, Pittsburgh Post-Gazette

WALT HANDELSMAN
Newsday

How to Field Dress a Donkey

PALIN

PALIN'S BID FOR V.P.

DARYL CAGLE
MSNBC.com

FREDERICK DELIGNE
Nice-Matin, France

ERIC ALLIE, Politicalcartoons.com

DARYL CAGLE
MSNBC.COM

MIKE KEEFE, Denver Post

NATE BEELER, Washington Examiner

JIMMY MARGULIES, The Record (NJ)

228

DANA SUMMERS
Orlando Sentinel

GARY VARVEL, Indianapolis Star

NATE BEELER, Washington Examiner

JOE HELLER, Green Bay Press Gazette

JOHN DARKOW, Columbia Daily Tribune (MO)

IT TAKES A WOMAN FROM AN ALASKAN VILLAGE TO RAISE YOUR PROSPECTS

STEVE BENSON
Arizona Republic

LARRY WRIGHT
Detroit News

R.J. MATSON
St. Louis Post Dispatch

www.electJohnMcCain.org/then_impeachhimrightawaysoSarahPalincanbePresident_in2008/

230

MICHAEL MCPARLANE, Politicalcartoons.com

TOO LATE TO THROW HER BACK NOW...

R.J. MATSON, St. Louis Post Dispatch

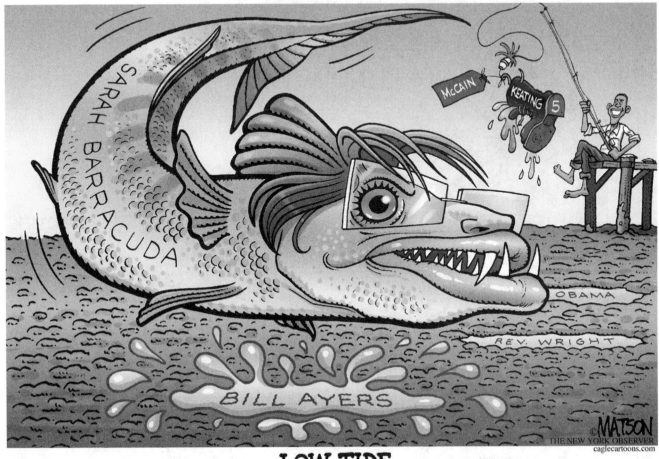

LOW TIDE

Biden's Bid for V.P.

Obama picked long-time Delaware Senator Joe Biden to be his running mate. Biden was seen as experienced in foreign policy, filling a gap in Obama's resume. Biden was also known for talking without thinking, and although he made some noteworthy gaffes on the campaign trail, Biden was largely ignored as Sarah Palin stole the veep spotlight.

R.J. MATSON, Roll Call

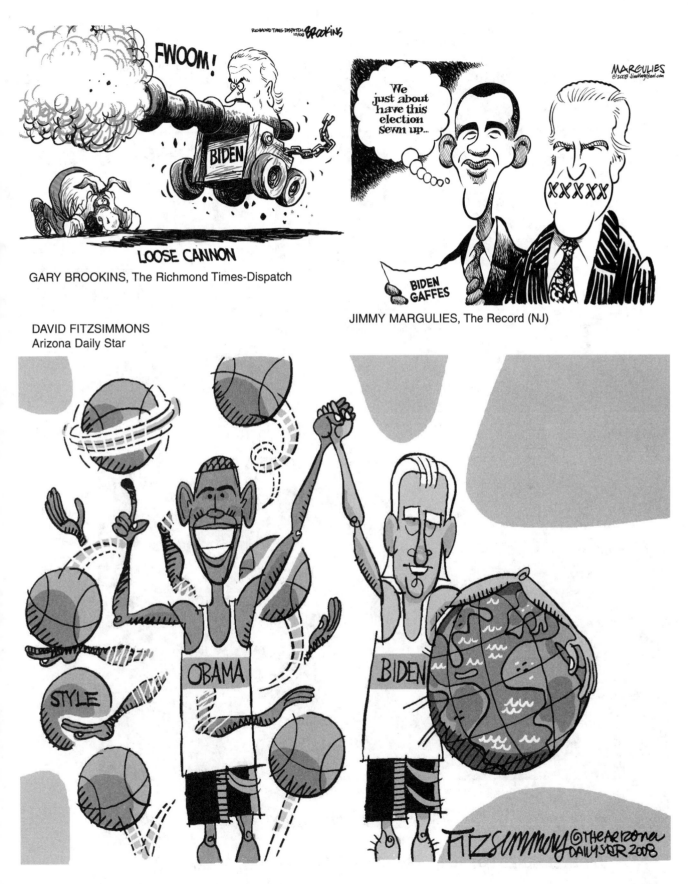

LOOSE CANNON
GARY BROOKINS, The Richmond Times-Dispatch

JIMMY MARGULIES, The Record (NJ)

DAVID FITZSIMMONS
Arizona Daily Star

©Taylor Jones

TAYLOR JONES, Politicalcartoons.com

SARAH PALIN

JOE BIDEN

R.J.
MATSON
New York
Observer

OBAMA
BIDEN

"JOE IS DETERMINED NOT TO BE THE FORGOTTEN MAN IN THIS ELECTION!"

236

JIMMY MARGULIES, The Record (NJ)

MIKE KEEFE, Denver Post

BOB ENGLEHART, Hartford Courant

BIDEN'S BID FOR V.P.

MEMORABLE LINES

WE WON'T HEAR AT TONIGHT'S DEBATE (OR WILL WE?)

R.J. MATSON, St. Louis Post Dispatch

THE NEXT MOONSHOT
JOHN DEERING, Arkansas Democrat Gazette

RANDY BISH
Pittsburgh Tribune-Review

MICHAEL RAMIREZ
Investors Business Daily

GARY MARKSTEIN

BIDEN'S BID FOR V.P.

ROBERT ARIAIL
The State, SC

MATT DAVIES, Journal News, NY

President Obama

Barack Obama won the presidential
election! The world cheered and
cartoonists took a step back to
contemplate the moment in history.

DARYL CAGLE, MSNBC.COM

HIST⬤RY

JIMMY MARGULIES, The Record (NJ)

BOB
GORRELL

PAT BAGLEY
Salt Lake
Tribune, UT

JOHN TREVER, Albuquerque Journal

JOHN SHERFFIUS, Boulder Daily Camera

BRUCE BEATTIE, Daytona News-Journal

PRESIDENCY

HOUSE

SENATE

JOE HELLER
Green Bay Press Gazette

PETAR PISMESTROVIC, Austria

BILL DAY
Memphis Commercial Appeal

CHUCK ASAY, Colorado Springs Gazette

DARYL CAGLE
MSNBC.COM

DAY ONE

MIKE LUCKOVICH
The Atlanta
Journal-Constitution

MIKE LUCKOVICH, The Atlanta Journal-Constitution

JACK OHMAN
Portland Oregonian

245

STEVE GREENBERG, Ventura County Star

MATT DAVIES, Journal News, NY

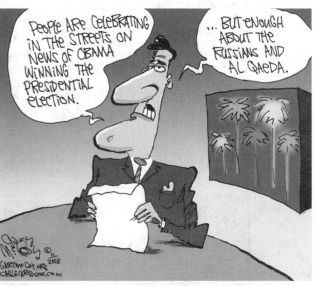

GARY MCCOY, Cagle Cartoons

THOMAS "TAB" BOLDT
Calgary Sun

IRAQ

ECONOMY

HOUSING

HUMAN RIGHTS

CHANGE

HOPE FOR A BRIGHT NEW FUTURE

OBAMA PRESIDENCY

RACIST LUNATIC FRINGE BACKLASH

© 2008 MONTE WOLVERTON

caglecartoons.com

MONTE WOLVERTON, Cagle Cartoons

247

STEPHANE PERAY
Thailand

PATRICK CHAPPATTE
International Herald Tribune

ERIC ALLIE
Cagle Cartoons

PAUL ZANETTI, Australia

PETAR PISMESTROVIC, Austria

PAUL ZANETTI, Australia

INGRID RICE, British Columbia, Canada

MIKE LANE, Cagle Cartoons

NOW GET OUT THERE AND FIND SOMEONE TO PAY FOR ALL THOSE PROMISES I MADE

RANDY BISH, Pittsburgh Tribune-Review

PAT BAGLEY, Salt Lake Tribune

Obama Makes History

Forty years after the death of Dr. Martin Luther King, Barack Obama made history as the first African-American to be elected President of the United States, inspiring millions around the world.

TAYLOR JONES
El Nuevo Dia
Puerto Rico

JIHO
France

ONE SMALL STEP FOR MAN...

ONE GIANT LEAP FOR MANKIND!

MLK

ABSENTEE VOTE

JOE HELLER
Green Bay
Press Gazette

CHANGE

YES, WE DID.

©MATSON
ST. LOUIS POST-DISPATCH
caglecartoons.com

R.J. MATSON, St. Louis Post Dispatch

DANA SUMMERS
Orlando Sentinel

WHERE'S LINCOLN?

NOT BACK FROM CHICAGO YET.

JEFF KOTERBA, Omaha World Herald

ADAM ZYGLIS
Buffalo News

MIKE KEEFE
Denver Post

NOVEMBER 5TH, 2008

HE'S BEEN LIKE THAT EVER SINCE ELECTION DAY 2008.

YESSSSSSS...

STEVE BREEN, San Diego Union Tribune

DAVID FITZSIMMONS, Arizona Daily Star

"Mr. President."

HENRY PAYNE, Detroit News

VINCE O'FARRELL, Illawarra Mercury, Australia

JOHN DARKOW, Columbia Daily Tribune (MO)

DWAYNE BOOTH, Mr. Fish

THOMAS "TAB" BOLDT
Calgary Sun
(Canada)

STEVE KELLEY, New Orleans Times-Picayune

JEFF PARKER, Florida Today

ED STEIN, Rocky Mountain News

JEFF STAHLER
Columbus Dispatch

In Memoriam

Memorial cartoons provide cartoonists with the rare opportunity of positive reflection on the lives of notable public figures – not to mention these are usually the most popular cartoons of the year. That's not to say that cartoon obits are always drawn in praise. This year, we lost many big names, from beloved actor Heath Ledger to dirty-mouthed George Carlin, old-timers Charlton Heston (yes, we can pry the gun from his cold, dead fingers now), Paul Newman, Bo Diddley, NBC's Tim Russert, Fox News' Tony Snow, Russia's Alexander Solzhenitsyn, and Senator Jesse Helms.

EVEL KNIEVEL 1938-2007

"PART THE PEARLY GATES FOR MR. HESTON, PLEASE!"

HENRY PAYNE
Detroit News

CHARLTON HESTON
1923-2008

GARY BROOKINS
The Richmond Times-Dispatch

STEVE BENSON, Arizona Republic

257

USSR

SOLZ-HENITSYN

HENRY PAYNE
Detroit News

ALEXANDER SOLZHENITSYN 1918–2008
BOB GORRELL

PAUL NEWMAN 1925–2008

ACTOR, ACTIVIST, PHILANTHROPIST

WHAT WE'VE GOT HERE, IS NO FAILURE TO APPRECIATE...

AND TWO INTENSELY BLUE STARS IN THE HOLLYWOOD SKY.

MARK STREETER
Savannah Morning News

CHARITY

Newman's own
JOHN SHERFFIUS, Boulder Daily Camera

YOU'RE IN

RECIPES

PETER BROELMAN, Australia

258

STEVE BENSON
Arizona Republic

HEATH LEDGER
1979~2008

MIKE LUCKOVICH
The Atlanta
Journal-Constitution

259

ROBERT ARIAIL
The State, SC

BOB GORRELL

WILLIAM F. BUCKLEY, JR. - 1925-2008

GARY BROOKINS
The Richmond Times-

William F. Buckley
1925-2008

GARY VARVEL
Indianapolis Star

JEFF STAHLER, Columbus Dispatch

SCOTT STANTIS, Birmingham News

JACK OHMAN
Portland Oregonian

BEFORE JIMI HENDRIX, ERIC CLAPTON, JEFF BECK, JIMMY PAGE AND KEITH RICHARDS, THERE WAS...

BO DIDDLEY : 1928–2008

CAMERON CARDOW
Ottawa Citizen (Canada)

MARSHALL RAMSEY, Clarion Ledger (MI)

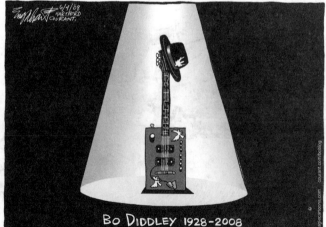

BOB ENGLEHART, Hartford Courant

DAVID FITZSIMMONS
Arizona Daily Star

HENRY PAYNE, Detroit News

"Do I have a perfect press secretary for you! . . . ."

MEET THE PRESS

MEET THE PRESS

TIM RUSSERT 1950-2008

R.J. MATSON, Roll Call

SURE GONNA MISS YA, TIM...

NBC

RICHARD CROWSON, Witchita Eagle

BILL SCHORR

Heaven Heaven Heaven

RUSSERT

"...IT ALL COMES DOWN TO THIS..."

STEVE BENSON, Arizona Republic

ROBERT ARIAIL, The State, SC

ADAM ZYGLIS, Buffalo News

SCOTT STANTIS
Birmingham News

BRIAN FAIRRINGTON, Cagle Cartoons

MIKE LUCKOVICH
The Atlanta
Journal-Constitution

CHIP BOK, Akron Beacon-Journal

JEFF STAHLER, Columbus Dispatch

GARY BROOKINS, The Richmond Times-Dispatch

STEVE BENSON, Arizona Republic

JERRY HOLBERT, Boston Herald

JOHN DEERING, Arkansas Democrat Gazette

MIKE KEEFE
Denver Post

Artists Index

You can see a complete archive of each cartoonist's work on our web site at www.cagle.com. Come take a look! Want to contact a cartoonist or ask for permission to reproduce a cartoon? Contact information for each cartoonist accompanies their cartoons on www.cagle.com.